# SOCIAL PSYCHOLOGY

# SOCIAL PSYCHOLOGY

## A Symbolic
## Interaction Perspective

J. D. CARDWELL

F. A. Davis Company, Philadelphia

*To H. Jeff Buttram, scholar and friend*

# FOREWORD

To introduce Jerry Cardwell's book on Symbolic Interactionism is a pleasure. We share an enthusiasm for the current and future utility of the approach.

This book presents, in an easy-to-read manner, the core dimensions of a symbolic interactionist interpretation of human behavior. The presentation synthesizes the contributions of early founders with the insights of modern scholars, to provide a contemporary interpretation which differs in significant details from some interpretations which treat symbolic interactionism as though its development stopped with the writings of Cooley, Mead and Dewey.

Human interaction involves biologic beings being social, or relating to each other. Cardwell discusses the relationship between these two basic factors, indicating that if the behavior of interacting individuals is in response to symbols as the symbolic interactionist maintains, man's biologic makeup must be of such a nature to permit this. Thus one of the most inflexible characteristics of man's biology is that it is flexible enough to permit individuals (but not subindividual elements) to respond to socially constructed and hence changeable symbols. He carefully avoids the use of what I have found it convenient to call "internalist" concepts which presumably identify internal causative factors, but in reality appear to be metaphysical constructs used by internalists to provide closure for their interpretations. Such closure seems to be unavailable when the internalist explanation incorporates only concepts which have empirical (physical) referents. Rather than talking about internal phenomena such as, for instance, a "mind," Cardwell talks about "minding symbols" or taking symbols into account. Actually, when metaphysical internalist constructs are translated into operationally defined researchable concepts, the phenomenon-of-attention usually turns out to be symbols. In essence, Cardwell says, "Let's concentrate our study on that to which you actually pay attention when you do research." Cardwell recognizes the advisability of not trying to construct a metaphysical "inner world." He is concerned rather with explaining the "socially constructed" social-symbolic world which man collectively creates. He is not concerned with what goes on inside individuals because he recognizes that the "inner world" of one individual and the social-symbolic world of interacting individuals are in fact different-level phenomena.

Cardwell illustrates the limitations of any internalist approach, emphasizing that individuals reciprocally influence each other through the medium of symbols. One individual influences another individual; some internal part of one individual does not contact the internal counterpart of the other individual. His explanations start outside the individual and work in, rather than attempting to start at some internal point and work out. With this initial orientation it is clear why he gives so much attention to the symbolic medium of interaction.

Having a biologic inheritance which permits flexible, malleable behavior is a necessary requisite for the most distinctive type of human creativity—creating symbols which have arbitrary, socially-constructed, consensual, changeable meaning, the totality of which is called culture. Meaning is thus created for the aspects of the empirical world that are taken into account. Such meaning is incorporated in symbols which have empirical referents. Other animals apparently also take the empirical world into account, although they do not do so symbolically by placing labels on it and then responding to the labels. It is man's use of symbols which distinguishes him from other animals, with the difference being a difference in kind rather than degree.

Man's most distinctive characteristic, however, is that he also creates symbol systems which symbolically preserve decisions which interacting individuals create to guide their future behavior. Men in interaction create symbolic models, ideals, or expectations to which they can compare their behavior and which can be consulted when future decisions are being made. Since such decisions have no empirical existence before they are socially created they involve a distinctive type of symbol, that is, symbols which have no empirical referent. These symbols are not distorted or "diseased," resulting from some type of ignorance, but rather are a distinctive symbolic creation. Such symbols are involved in religion, various art forms, games, poems, jokes, symphonies and mathematical and algebraic systems. The importance of behavior which is in response to these symbols is suggested by the intensity with which individuals may respond to a poem or other work of art which does not refer to just some aspect of the empirical world but rather is a symbolic creation per se. Cardwell's discussions of such symbols emphasizes their high saliency in human behavior.*

This creative potential, which stems from man's ability to create, preserve, transmit and respond to symbols, has been handled inadequately by most social scientists. Cardwell helps to remedy this deficiency.

Cardwell points out that decision making involves taking into account a synthesized configuration of cultural elements, including value definitions, norm definitions, self definitions, role definitions, definitions of the situation, temporal definitions and spatial definitions. The meaning of these cultural aspects is learned. The manner in which humans engage in behavior related to these symbols is learned. Socialization (the learning process) is an important human process, emphasized throughout the book.

His analysis of the manner in which relevant definitions are synthesized in making specific decisions, which are in turn assessed and reassessed as interaction episodes unfold, provides understanding of the dynamic flexibility of human interaction, which contrasts with the greater rigidity of the behavior of lower-level (non-symbol-using) animals. The approach could be called a "cluster," "configurational," or "reciprocal influence" approach. It involves basic core dimensions plus reinforcing, supporting variables which are harmony producing. It also involves inhibiting, contradictory, disorganizing variables, such as cognitive dissonance, which provide the conflict dimensions of every sociocultural system.

The resistance to change of any social system is related to the rigidity with which its members accept important definitions. "Cultural inertia" is social not biologic in origin. Behavior can be changed if those involved accept new definitions. However, achieving such change is difficult for high saliency definitions. With reference to certain racial characteristics discussed by Cardwell, it would almost seem easier to change the biology than to change the definitions thereof.

The overall emphasis is that the behavior of humans is in response to symbols, rather than to the unlabeled or unsymboled "raw" world. Man symbolically creates his behavior in the form of models, or plans of action, blueprints, or scripts, before he physically enacts or engages in behavior which corresponds to the symbolic model. He, of course, creates emergent aspects of his behavior as he engages therein. Behavior is not

---

* A few social scientists are starting to point out that there are interesting parallels between what the social scientist calls "symbols" (especially those with nonempirical referents) and what the religionist calls "spiritual." Each may be talking about somewhat the same thing. Each emphasizes the importance of this symbolic-"spiritual" aspect of human behavior.

all prescripted or preprogrammed. Certain goals are established, for instance, even after the race has started.

In addition to being in response to symbols, the behavior of the individual is relative to the intended audience (s) , including those physically present, and those only symbolically present who may be living, dead or as yet unborn. The audience may include those waiting in the wings, so to speak, to come on stage and get into the act, various "back-up" teams, and others whose supporting vote or veto is taken into account. This interaction aspect is summarized in the statement that "you can't behave in a human way all by yourself."

All of these factors get synthesized or integrated in terms of the situation or the stage in which (upon which) the episode occurs.

When Cardwell uses the term "symbolic interaction" he incorporates all of these interrelated components. The symbolic interactionist interpretation of human behavior then incorporates multi-dimensional high-complexity level phenomena.

Cardwell accomplishes his goal of presenting basic points of his approach in an easily-understood manner, building systematically from chapter to chapter on the previously established points or premises. The cumulative theoretical statements help the student to know where he has been, or to recognize the symbolic ground he has traversed. The text itself thus provides a brief illustration of the theory-building process of integrating concepts and premises which is discussed in the last chapter. The last chapter also includes some of the methodological problems involved in the study of the complex phenomena of human interaction.

In view of the previous relationships I have enjoyed with Jerry Cardwell, the publication of this book is a source of personal satisfaction. A combination of a satisfying interpersonal relationship with a rewarding academic relationship compounds the satisfaction, a fact which in itself illustrates one of Cardwell's underlying premises, that is, that how one individual behaves provides rewards for others.

This publication is an effort to expand and clarify basic dimensions of symbolic interactionism. In an age of various so-called "mind-expanding" endeavors, it has been a delightful experience to sense the "mind-expanding" experience which Cardwell has had in his encounter with symbolic interactionism. His interest in understanding and expanding the approach is reflected in his writing. It is hoped that the reader will capture some of Cardwell's enthusiasm for the subject.

Glenn M. Vernon
The University of Utah
Salt Lake City

# PREFACE

This small book was written with two major purposes in mind: (1) to introduce the beginning student of sociology or social psychology to the basic assumptions and principles of symbolic interaction theory; and (2) to present the theory in such a manner that the student will know where his study of the general orientation of symbolic interaction theory has taken him, while at the same time providing the student with the flexibility of constant review of major concepts.

In order to achieve these stated purposes, the presentation of the material contained herein can be identified as one of discussion and conceptual derivation. Each topic discussed in the book is set forth in a manner which, while not designed to conform to a system of logical deduction, is believed to be conceptually consistent. In a summary of each chapter the topics covered in preceding discussions are presented a second time in the form of statements which are, I believe, conceptually consistent one with the other. Again, no claim to the canons of logical deduction is made. This method of presentation allows the beginning student to refer to previous chapter summaries in order to reorient himself should he become perplexed over the material at any given point in the text. Furthermore, the theoretical statements outlined at the end of each chapter are arranged to form a conceptually consistent outline of symbolic interaction theory.

The whole of symbolic interaction theory is not treated in this book. Such a task is beyond the intended scope of the present endeavor. This work discusses only those areas of the theory which are typically covered in conventional introductory texts for sociology and social psychology. This is done in the belief that symbolic interaction theory as it is discussed in the general sociological literature is beyond the full comprehension of the uninitiated student, and that a simpler presentation of the essentials of the theory would better serve the purposes for which this book is intended.

Chapter 1 is concerned with the symbolic and biologic foundations of human behavior. These topics were chosen primarily because of the author's belief that they represent what Furfey* would label the "metasociological" assumptions of the theory. The differentiation of empirical and nonempirical referents is taken from Vernon's† work, and the device of levels of abstraction emerged from discussions with Professor James Dorsett of the Department of Sociology at Virginia Polytechnic Institute. Chapter 2 illustrates the nature of the social meaning of symbols by examination of value definitions and the impact of them on human behavior insofar as they imply plans of action, that is, expectations for normative behavior. Chapters 3 and 4 deal with the definition of the situation on two different levels, the social and cultural, respectively. Chapter 4 relies heavily, as does much of the book, on the thinking and writing of Professor Glenn M. Vernon. Chapter 5 illustrates the nature of the self, the concept of role, and the interrelationships between them. Role playing and role taking are discussed and differentiated. A collection of the theoretical statements into a conceptual whole is presented at the end of Chapter 5.

Chapter 6 presents a brief discussion of theory and methods as they relate to the discussions in Chapters 1 through 5. This chapter emphasizes the importance of the process of careful integration of concepts and premises which is necessary for theory building. The discussion of measurement, while somewhat more difficult than other parts of the text, should prove useful if the book is utilized in a course other than at the introductory level.

Robert King Merton‡ once said that "No man knows fully what has shaped his thinking," and such is usually considered true. It seems to me, however, that there are certain areas of knowledge in which an individual can be relatively certain as to particular scholars who have influenced his thinking. For this author such a scholar is Dr. Glenn M. Vernon, who is presently Chairman, Department of Sociology, the University of Utah. During my studies under Dr. Vernon as a graduate student at the University of Maine, the vast majority of my thinking on symbolic interaction theory took place. Under his careful guidance I was, I believe, able to develop a grasp of the nature of the theoretical orienta-

---

* Furfey, Paul H.: *The Scope and Method of Sociology: A Metasociological Treatise.* New York: Harper, 1953.

† Vernon, Glenn M.: *Human Interaction: An Introduction to Sociology.* New York: Ronald Press, Inc., 1965.

‡ Merton, Robert K.: *Social Theory and Social Structure.* New York: The Free Press, 1957.

tion. Thus, references to Dr. Vernon's works are made throughout the text, for as Merton says, it is difficult to always give credit where it is due.

In order to avoid the possibility of such an event, I have taken no chances and have cited Dr. Vernon liberally.

J. D. C.
The University of Utah
Salt Lake City

# ACKNOWLEDGMENTS

Intellectual debts cannot be repaid; at best they can only be acknowledged. Dr. H. Jeff Buttram of the University of Alabama opened my eyes to the exciting enterprise the sociological endeavor is. Dr. Stephen L. Finner, now of the University of Delaware, supplied motivation, know-how, and a keen sociological mind during my early graduate education. His time, thoughts, and energy were willingly offered, and utilized. Dr. David L. Klemmack of the Virginia Polytechnic Institute and State University provided insightful criticisms, suggestions, and an adept eye for manuscript review. Dr. Glenn M. Vernon of the University of Utah read the manuscript from cover to cover and offered numerous criticisms and suggestions for revisions. The book is indeed in his debt. Mr. Joe Witcher, Vice President and Editor of F. A. Davis, provided professional assistance of a high calibre. He was always ready when problems arose. To my wife, Nancy, who typed, read, retyped, and reread the manuscript from beginning to end, I am very grateful. Finally, I would like to extend appreciation to Jody Scranton. She guided a relatively naive fellow through the jungle of problems associated with publishing with professional expertise.

The authors and publishers of the quoted material found in this text graciously gave their permission to reprint. Specific acknowledgment of their permission is given with the references.

# CONTENTS

# 6

# SOCIAL PSYCHOLOGY

Society is "my representation"—something dependent upon the activity of consciousness—in quite a different sense from that in which the external world is. For the other individual has for me the same reality which I have for myself, and this reality is very different from that of a material thing.[1]

GEORG SIMMEL

Our problems are man-made; therefore they can be solved by man.[2]

JOHN F. KENNEDY

# 1

# SYMBOLIC AND BIOLOGIC
# FOUNDATIONS OF
# HUMAN BEHAVIOR

In order for the sociologist to formulate a theoretical orientation to the processes of human behavior, he must first delimit his area of concern insofar as it relates to human beings in general. In the process of specifying his domain of attention he will, of necessity, exclude certain kinds of behavior, and questions about behavior, from consideration. Thus he will—in the sense that some human phenomena are not made the object of study—limit the kinds of answers he can provide about human interaction.[3] The approach of the symbolic interactionist is not different in this regard.*

The assumptions of this approach are such that emphasis is placed upon the cultural rather than the biologic aspect of human behavior. This does not mean that biology does not influence human behavior, or that biologic influences are unimportant. It simply means that the sociologist selectively studies the cultural aspects of man and the biologist, for example, selectively studies the biologic aspects of man. Thus, an initial assumption of the symbolic interactionist is that human behavior is cultural in origin, and further, that human behavior is social in its consequences.[4]

---

* This is true of all scientific enterprises. Even the fact of subdivision or specialization within disciplines contributes to the conscription of the focus of attention. However, the scientific approach has been assumed to be the one utilized by the sociologist and reference is made to the differing kinds of answers the scientific and nonscientific approaches may yield. For an excellent discussion of this problem, see: Glenn M. Vernon: "Communication Between Theologians and Social Scientists in Research" in *Review of Religious Research*, Winter, 1966, pp. 93-100.

We learn to be humans from contact with other human beings. If social behavior is defined as the process of two or more individuals taking each other into account, it becomes clear that the initial assumption means that without extended contact with other humans, we would not act in a manner that is usually thought to represent humanness. Examples of the manner in which this assumption holds have been documented in the general sociological literature.[5]

Clearly, to say that we learn to be humans from contact with other humans is not, in and of itself, a new statement. Furthermore, one might be prompted to state that the same is true with animals other than human beings. To be sure, the majority of animals are taught to behave in a manner that is compatible with their species. It is well accepted by both social and natural scientists that wild carnivores are taught how to hunt and kill for their livelihood; young apes are socialized in the correct ways of behaving; and certain insects are organized into independent units with divisions of labor.[6] It is our contention, however, that to move from this single similarity (the similarity of learning regardless of processual considerations, that is, whether the learning is by imitation, repetition, or abstract reasoning), to the assertion that learning to behave in lower animals is much like learning to behave in a human manner would be a grave, if not naive, mistake. Human beings learn to behave in a cultural manner by traversing an entirely different route than other animals.

## SYMBOLS, REFERENTS, AND CONSENSUAL MEANING

As stated previously, an initial assumption of the sociologist is that human behavior is cultural in the majority of its aspects. Proceeding from that assumption, the symbolic interactionist maintains that human behavior which is identified as cultural is in response to stimuli—stimuli which are identified as symbols.

A moment's reflection is all we need to realize that if we could not agree among ourselves as to what an object "is," we would likewise be at a loss to communicate with each other concerning the nature of the object. Actually, we rarely do agree among ourselves as to what a thing "is." The usual pattern is that we agree concerning the meaning of symbols. Symbols, as we shall use the term, stand for, or represent, something else.[7] A symbol may be a word, a gesture, a facial expression, or a combination of these. The "thing" which the symbol stands for (or to which it refers) is termed a *referent*.

Symbols are part of our empirical reality. By "empirical reality" is meant that part of our environment which exists outside of the individual, and is available to at least one of his five senses. Thus, we can

4

see the written word or hear the spoken word; we can observe the gesture, just as we can see the facial expression. In this sense then, symbols—as things which stand for something else—are a part of our empirical reality.

Unlike symbols, referents may be a part of either our "empirical" or our "nonempirical" reality, that is, referents may or may not be available to the five senses. The thing associated with the symbol "chair" is an example of an empirical referent, and the thing associated with the symbol "beauty" is an example of a nonempirical referent. While the chair exists in empirical reality, beauty, of course, does not, but resides "in the eyes of the beholder."

Thus we can say that symbols are empirical. We can also state that the things to which symbols refer, that is, referents, can be either empirical or nonempirical.[8] Examples of the former are the things to which the symbols "book," "typewriter," and "television" refer, while examples of the latter are the "things" to which the symbols "goodness," "love," and "God" refer.

Symbols represent categories.[9] Obviously, all books are not exactly alike. Nor does the symbol God refer to the same "thing" in every society. Symbols then, refer us to a general category of referents, the range of which may be quite large. Symbols alert us to the general configuration into which the "thing" falls.

Humans learn the meaning attached to symbols and their accompanying referents. We are not born into the world as functioning cultural human beings. The symbolic interactionist maintains that there is no inherent relationship between the symbols used and what they stand for.[10] A given symbol may stand for anything. Symbols come to refer to certain things as a result of a group of people arriving at consensus as to what a symbol is to stand for, or represent. Knowledge of group consensus of the meaning of symbols is acquired via the socialization process. Through socialization we acquire the unique attributes of human beings; socialization involves human interaction, and human interaction is symbolic interaction. Since the meaning of any symbol is not an inherent quality of that symbol, man decides what its meaning shall be. We learn, that is, we are socialized, into being cultural beings. Taking on the attributes of a socialized human requires learning the meaning of the symbols utilized in the adult world, that is, learning the connection between the symbol and the thing to which it refers.* We learn the *cultural* meaning of the symbols adult humans use in their interaction with each other. If one fails for some reason—either biologic

---

* The "things" to which some symbols refer do not, by definition, exist in *our* objective reality. We do not know, and cannot know by using the scientific method, if they exist at all. In fact, we cannot even address the question. For that reason, the word *things* will be enclosed in quotation marks when referring to referents of such symbols.

or social—to learn the conventional meanings attached to symbols, he is unable to assume adequately the role of a socialized human. Lindesmith and Strauss have made this quite clear in their work, and because of its relevance it deserves extensive quotation at this point.[11]

> To teach anyone the conventional meaning of a word is to teach him how to act or think with reference to the object or the concept to which the word refers. The meanings of words are not locked up in dictionaries, but are found in people's acts.
> The child's learning of language is not merely an intellectual matter. Language puts the child in touch with his parents and playmates in new and significant ways and initiates his acquisition of broader and more specialized perspectives. It introduces him to new pleasures and satisfactions, and also creates a great many new needs and problems. Through learning a language he learns of the rules and standards that regulate social relations and develops ideas of morality and religious matters. Language is also the means whereby he is gradually prepared for and later inducted into the roles which he is destined to play and through which he learns to grasp the viewpoints and understand the feelings and sentiments of other persons. *By means of language he becomes aware of his own identity as a person and as a member of groups in which he seeks status, security, and self-expression and which in turn makes demands upon him.*

Symbols, then, have no inherent meaning. They acquire their meaning through the process of consensus of the human actors who use them. Were humans not to arrive at consensus as to the meaning of symbols, social interaction as it has been defined (see page 4) would be impossible. We could neither understand nor anticipate the behavior of others, and they could neither understand nor anticipate our behavior. The fact that humans can reach some manner of consensus as to the meaning of the symbols—and the referents relative thereto—is crucial in terms of understanding the separation between humans as cultural animals and the remainder of the animal world. Only human beings have the ability to communicate symbolically. This fact alone accounts for the differences between human and subhuman behavior.

## LEVELS OF SYMBOLIC ABSTRACTION

It has been stated that only humans communicate symbolically. The cultural nature of symbolic learning involves coming to consensus as to the meaning of symbols. The process of arriving at a consensual understanding of the meaning of symbols involves the individual's ability to make the connection between symbols and referents at different levels of abstraction. We are referring, at this point, to three stages of what we will identify as abstract representation. The individual completes each of the three stages of abstract representation during the process of socialization. The initial stage is the level of *general abstraction*; the second the level of *intermediate abstraction*; the third is the level of *specific abstraction*. While the nature of the language used to identify the stages suggests otherwise (general, intermediate, specific), the movement through the various levels of abstraction represents a process of increased sophistication in terms of abstract thinking.

What we are referring to at present is the abstract nature of symbols through the use of which man can relate various concepts that exist in a symbolic environment.[12] Without the ability to do this, abstract thinking which characterizes the human being would be unknown. It should be made clear at the outset, however, that these stages are not completely independent in relation to each other, and that the stages do not necessarily form a linear sequence. Although the sequence is not necessarily linear, it is conceptually so.

The newborn infant is exposed to a multitude of symbols and their referents by his parents and other adults. Over a period of time the child comes to make the symbolic link between the symbols and the objects to which they refer. Most assuredly, the initial connection between symbol and referent is a tenuous one. At first the child relates the symbol to any object that has the general characteristics of the thing. This stage of symbol learning we shall identify as the level of general abstraction in which the range of referents to which the symbol refers is broad, or general. According to Lindesmith and Strauss:[13]

> When the child first discovers adult words, he does not employ them to specify precisely the same objects that are referred to by adults. To put this into common-sense terms, the child does not at first use adult words with their correct adult meaning—the infant, in fact, applies sounds and home-made words to objects long before he masters adult words. It is out of these initial vocal references that his ability to use adult words correctly eventually develops. . . . *The child sometimes uses adult words to designate objects outside the adult definition, and sometimes he does not use the word to designate enough objects. Some words he uses more widely than we do, others more narrowly.*

Thus the connection between symbol and referent is initially one of general abstraction, or general abstract representation. However, as

Lindesmith and Strauss point out, "When the child has managed to discover that every object has a name he has taken a conspicuous step toward learning parental speech."[14] This is no less true because of the broad category of meaning the child attaches to each symbol. The range of referents to which a symbol may refer is extremely large at first, perhaps with referents that are not vaguely related to the symbol included in the general configuration. Even so, the child has taken a significant step in the process of communication with his fellow humans. Of course, as the child grows older he will exclude some referents from connection with the symbol and, in all probability, will include others which he had heretofore excluded from the relationship. Through this process the symbol chair, for example, comes to refer to the general category of chair, and many refinements are made by modifying the symbol to refer to specific kinds of referents. Under the general category of chair, specific modifications such as "easy chair," "kitchen chair," "lawn chair," take place. This level of abstraction we shall label as the intermediate stage of abstract representation.

Using symbols involves more than just the application of labels or titles to things. Symbols also provide plans of action.[15] Thus, when we attach the label "chair" to something, we are providing two essential pieces of information about the object. First, we are providing information as to what the thing is, and second, we are providing information as to what one is expected to do in connection with the object, for example, if it is a chair, one is to sit in it.

This process of symbolic refinement enables the individual to anticipate the uses of each type of referent and the behavior expected of him relative to various situations. The referent becomes an important variable in terms of defining proper behavior. We call this level of abstraction the specific level of abstract representation. At this stage the individual has not only labeled referents under a general symbolic heading and made specific modifications relative thereto, he has come to associate plans of action with the symbols in their more specific symbolic form. Thus, on the basis of symbolic refinement, he is able to represent situations before he encounters them and visualize the kinds of objects that will be present, and the expected behavior relative to the objects. He can, in addition, anticipate the behavior of others.

## SIGNS AND SYMBOLS

In order to understand better the relationship between a symbol and what it represents, further distinctions regarding the definition of symbols must be made. Recall that symbols are things that stand for something else. Recall further that the meaning of the symbol does not reside within it but, rather, the meaning a symbol comes to have is a result of consensus as to its meaning on the part of humans who use it. The symbol "book" does not, by its very nature, refer to a specific referent. "Book" comes to represent a thing with pages and printed words placed between two covers only because man has, collectively, agreed that such is the meaning the symbol should have. Man could have used an entirely different symbol to represent the thing (s) conventionally referred to as book (s). It is at this juncture that the essential symbolic nature of man resides. Man is capable of deciding the meaning any given symbol will have. He is also capable, unlike other animals, of arbitrarily changing the meaning of a symbol by consensus with his fellow humans. Subhuman animals are incapable of accomplishing such a feat because animals other than humans respond to "signs," not symbols.

It is essential to understand the difference between a "sign" and a "symbol."[16] A sign has meaning only in concrete situations. The meaning of the sign is fixed and unchanging; it is set within a given situational context and meaning relative to it cannot be changed arbitrarily. A symbol, however, is a completely arbitrary thing. The meaning attached to a symbol can be changed as the situation in which it is used changes. Further, the single symbol can be made to stand for a wide variety of phenomena. The sign, on the other hand, does not have this quality. Thus, man can decide that a certain sound means to run for cover at one time, and as the situation changes, decide that the identical sound means to run into the open and attract attention. Lower animals cannot change the meaning of signs as man can change the meaning of symbols. Once a sign comes to have a certain meaning for other animals, the meaning is fixed and not subject to reinterpretation.*

Miller has provided an excellent illustration of the significance of symbolic communication as differentiated from sign communication:[17]

> Words cannot be distinguished from other stimuli on the basis of the representative role or their organization into patterns. What then, is the distinguishing mark of a verbal stimulus? One possible distinction is that words have an arbitrary significance. Words signify only what we have learned they signify. The fact that we say "chair" and not "Stuhl" is a matter of social coincidence. In contrast, the association between the light rays reflected from a chair

---

* The behavior of animals (and presumably the meaning of signs to which they respond) *can* be changed by *man* through the conditioning process. However, animals alone cannot consensually change the meaning of a sign.

and the chair itself is not arbitrary. Verbal signs that are organized into linguistic systems are usually called verbal symbols.

The arbitrary nature of a verbal stimulus is clear when we consider the role of learning. In general we learn to repeat those acts which are rewarded. If bumping into a chair is never rewarded, we soon stop behaving that way and start walking around it. In such cases the nature of the physical situation ensures that our responses develop in a certain way. Our responses to the word "chair," however, develop differently. In order that we learn to respond correctly to the word "chair," *it is necessary for another organism to intervene and reward us each time we respond correctly.* Since the intervening organism can reward a range of possible responses, the choice of the sound pattern "chair" is quite arbitrary.*

Thus we have discussed symbols, referents, and the consensual nature of symbolic communication (interaction). Earlier, we stated that human behavior which is identified as cultural is in response to symbols. Hopefully, such is apparent at this point. It would not be an overstatement to maintain that man knows himself culturally through identification of the labels which others apply to him.[18] We will have more to say in this regard in Chapter 3. It follows from this that we know our friends, as well as our foes, only insofar as we label them (symbolically) as such. We react to the labels we believe others have applied to us.[19]

We will conclude this discussion with an extensive quote from one of the precursors of symbolic interaction theory. Ernst Cassirer clearly recognized the importance of symbols for the life of man, and his comments are particularly instructive at this point in our discussion.[20]

In the human world we find a new characteristic which appears to be the distinctive mark of human life. The functional circle of man is not only quantitatively enlarged; it also has undergone a qualitative change. Man has, as it were, discovered a new method of adapting himself to his environment. Between the receptor system and the effector system, which are to be found in all animal species, we find in man a third link which we may describe as the symbolic system. This new acquisition transforms the whole of human life. As compared with the other animals man lives not in a broader

---

* As will become apparent in Chapter 5, it is not necessary for an "organism" to intercede and reward us each time we respond in the appropriate manner. The main point here, however, is that the connection between symbol and referent and, subsequently, "correct" behavior, is not God-given but arbitrary. It is a social convention.

reality; he lives, so to speak, in a new *dimension* of reality. There is an unmistakable difference between organic reaction and human responses. . . .

From the point of view at which we have just arrived we may correct and enlarge the classical definition of man. In spite of all the efforts of modern irrationalism this definition of man as *animal rationale* has not lost its force. Rationality is indeed an inherent feature of all human activities. Mythology itself is not simply a crude mass of superstitions or gross delusions. It is not merely chaotic, for it possesses a systematic or conceptual form. But on the other hand, it would be impossible to characterize the structure of myth as rational. Language has often been identified with reason, or with the very source of reason. But it is easy to see that this definition fails to cover the whole field. It is a *pars pro toto:* it offers a part for the whole. . . .

Reason is a very inadequate term with which to comprehend the forms of man's cultural life in all their richness and variety. But all these forms are symbolic forms. Hence, instead of defining man as *animal rationale,* we should define him as *animal symbolicum.* By doing so we can designate his specific difference, and we can understand the new way open to man—the way to civilization.

Like all other approaches to the study of man, the perspective of the symbolic interactionist sensitizes the social psychologist to certain ways of viewing human behavior. The decision to take this approach limits the kinds of behavior the sociologist can pay attention to, and in doing so, excludes certain kinds of answers from his capability. By taking the symbolic interactionist approach to the study of man, the researcher commits himself to the study of cultural aspects of man's behavior.

We have identified symbols as things which stand for, or represent, something else. The things which the symbols stand for or represent we have identified as referents. Referents, as we have identified them, can be either empirical or nonempirical. We further distinguished between signs and symbols and indicated that man's ability to communicate symbolically represents an essential difference between the reality of man's cultural behavior and the behavior of other animals.

From the discussion presented in this chapter, the following statements concerning symbolic interaction theory can be set forth. They are not intended to conform to the principles of logical deduction but, rather, are intended to be compatible with the conceptual development presented in this chapter.

11

1. Human behavior is cultural in the majority of its aspects.

2. Human behavior which is identified as cultural is in response to symbols.*

3. Humans are able to utilize symbols insofar as some consensus as to their meaning is reached.

4. Symbolic meaning is learned, that is, it is acquired through the process of socialization.

## BIOLOGIC FOUNDATIONS OF HUMAN BEHAVIOR

We have been talking thus far about the cultural foundation of human behavior and have suggested that man's behavior has a cultural base. A further illustration of the approach we have outlined is contained in a discussion of the biologic bases of human behavior. As previously stated, it is not our position that biology is unimportant to human behavior. It is maintained, however, that biologic aspects of man are not the appropriate area of inquiry for the symbolic interactionist.

Heredity and genetic transmission obviously play an important part in determining physical appearance of the human animal. The basic principles of biologic inheritance in the human are not unlike these factors in other animals. Genetic transmission determines such characteristics of the individual as sex, eye color, amount and texture of hair, and pigmentation of the skin. Generally speaking, however, important though these factors are in terms of man's potential to become biologically human, they do not have the effect of limiting or determining his cultural behavior (given the assumption that the individual is normal in his biologic makeup).

Such factors as eye and skin color, and amount and texture of hair, have consequences for cultural behavior only insofar as they are given symbolic meaning. There is nothing in the biologic makeup of hazel eyes, for instance, that makes them superior to blue or brown eyes. The color of an individual's eyes would be important for cultural behavior if, and only if, color of eyes was defined as important by man through symbolic interaction. Perhaps the most important biologic characteristics of man for the sociologist are those factors which are usually attributed to racial differences. Presented below is a brief outline of racial biologic differences.[21]

---

* These first two assumptions approximate Rose's initial assumption discussed in "A Systematic Summary of Symbolic Interaction Theory" in *Human Behavior and Social Processes*, Arnold M. Rose (ed.). Boston: Houghton Mifflin Co., 1962, pp. 3-19.

1. *Skin Color.* The color of the skin is the most obvious distinguishing characteristic of race. It is also the least reliable.

2. *Eye Color.* This classification is open to many of the same errors and discrepancies as skin color. Color of the eye (or rather of the iris) is satisfactory for comparative purposes only within the Caucasoid race, since all non-Caucasoid peoples have either a dark brown or black iris.

3. *Stature.* This category includes height and weight and ratios between them. Stature is subject to considerable variations because of environmental and dietary differences. A superior diet and standard of living will appreciably raise the height and weight of a given population over several generations.

4. *Hair Texture.* The texture of the hair in cross section under a microscope is an important criterion of racial differences. This trait is almost completely determined by genes and hence is distinctly "racial" in character.

5. *Head Shape.* The shape of the head is useful in distinguishing between subraces within a single racial group. The cephalic index is the principal measurement of head shape and is found by multiplying the width of the head by 100 and then dividing the product by the length of the head. Caucasoid, Mongoloid, and Negroid groups cannot be set off from each other accurately on the basis of cephalic index.

6. *Body Hair.* Members of the Caucasoid race have considerably more hair on their bodies than Negroid and Mongoloid peoples.

7. *Epicanthic Fold.* This trait refers to a fold of skin in the inner upper eyelid, characteristic of the Mongoloid peoples of continental Asia and some small groups. This factor is also affected by the genes and not by environmental influences.

8. *Blood Type.* Human beings also differ in the composition of their blood. There are four principle types of blood, known as O, A, B, and AB. There are no absolute differences in which one race is all of one blood type and another all of another type.

It is true that biologic inheritance influences each of the above characteristics. However, not one of the eight factors listed determines, or limits, man's cultural behavior. Of the racial characteristics identified, none are inherently "good" or "bad," or "superior" or "inferior." A decision as to the relative worth of these factors must be made by attaching meaning to the symbols which stand for, or represent, these attributes. It is precisely this symbolic meaning associated with these attributes that makes race an important area of study for the sociologist. As should be clear, this is because there is a distinct difference between (1) biologic factors per se and, (2) what anyone chooses to do about them. The fact that biologic differences between the races do occur is not the crucial factor, but rather, the manner in which man symbolically labels his differential biologic makeup—and that this is a cultural process— is important to the social psychologist.

The biology of the Negro which determines that he will be born with brown eyes, brown skin, and less body hair than the Caucasian is not, *unless socially defined as such*, inferior to the range of eye colors the white man has, or his skin color or more hairy condition. Our point here is that without the ability to communicate symbolically about his biologic makeup and arrive at differential definitions relative thereto, man would be unable to assume value positions that influence the manner in which he relates to his biologic state. We will have more to say about value definitions in a later chapter of this book.

The perspective of the symbolic interactionist does not allow the social scientist to fall into the "semantic trap" so often encountered in the social and behavioral sciences when attempting to explain, or predict, human behavior.[22] We can see, and sometimes hear, behavior that is usually thought to represent sexual, emotional, or instinctual behavior. However, if we make the biologic analogy, we will eventually find ourselves postulating "sex drives," "emotions," or "instincts" as "things" which reside inside the individual as the cause of the observed behavior. We would then attempt to explain or predict behavior on the basis of these metaphysical "things" within the individual as causal agents.* Aside from the fact that analogies are usually misrepresentations of reality, these things—sex drives, emotions, instincts—do not meet the criteria of being empirical. That is, they exist inside of the individual (see footnote) and are not available to the five senses. The symbols to which the symbolic interactionist pays attention are empirical and it is on the basis of observation of symbolic behavior that he attempts to explain, predict, or otherwise account for man's actions.

The position set forth here is, in summary, consistent with that of Vernon:[23]

> Biologically, the human body is a multi-potential. We could not use symbols in the manner we have decribed if this were not so. Such individual features as sex, body build, racial characteristics,

---

* Actually, it would be more accurate to say these "things" are *presumed* to exist, or are believed to exist, by those who use these concepts.

and capacity to learn, as well as the usual complement of internal organs and glands, are biologically given. These, however, provide the foundation for subsequent social behavior, they do not determine it. . . .

Neither biological inheritance or social experience is more important than the other in human behavior. Each is a necessary ingredient of the behavior equation, and each has a reciprocal relationship with the other. It is important, however, to recognize the fact to which sociology sensitizes us, that man is more than just a biological being—he is also a social being.

We are now in a position to present another statement concerning symbolic interaction theory.

5. In the sense that human interaction is symbolic interaction, it is considered noninstinctive. By noninstinctive is meant that human manipulation of symbols is not regulated, or directed, by any biologic condition within the individual.

## SUMMARY

The reader may, at this point, believe that some rather simple concepts have been over explained or over emphasized. There is good reason for such to be the case. In the conduct of sociological research, the symbolic interactionist, because he is aware of the symbolic nature of human interaction, does not leave the meaning of the symbols he employs in his work unspecified. As a result, the reader of a work utilizing this approach can proceed with the smallest possible amount of confusion as to what the writer is talking about. The specification of the meaning of the symbols he employs also aids the writer in clarifying for himself the nature of his work. In addition, a clear understanding of the materials presented in this chapter is a prerequisite for an adequate understanding of later chapters, and for that reason the concepts set forth here have been emphasized.

## CUMULATIVE THEORETICAL STATEMENTS

1. Human behavior is cultural in the majority of its aspects.

2. Human behavior which is identified as cultural is in response to symbols.

3. Humans are able to utilize symbols insofar as some consensus as to their meaning is reached.

4. Symbolic meaning is learned, that is, it is acquired through the process of socialization.

5. In the sense that human interaction is symbolic interaction, it is considered noninstinctive. By noninstinctive is meant that human manipulation of symbols is not regulated, or directed, by any biologic condition within the individual.

## NOTES AND REFERENCES

1. GEORG SIMMEL: "How Is Society Possible?" in *Philosophy of the Social Sciences*. Maurice Natanson (ed.). Copyright 1963, pp. 73-92. Material reprinted by permission of Random House, Inc., New York, New York.

2. JOHN F. KENNEDY: *Words to Remember*. New York: Hallmark, 1967, p. 41.

3. GLENN M. VERNON: *Human Interaction: An Introduction to Sociology*. New York: Ronald Press, Inc., 1965.

4. ARNOLD M. ROSE (ed.) : *Human Behavior and Social Processes*. Boston: Houghton Mifflin Co., 1962.

5. KINGSLEY DAVIS: "Final Note on a Case of Extreme Isolation" in *American Journal of Sociology* 52:432-437, 1947.

6. For a good general survey of the place of nonsymbolic factors in the various social psychological approaches, see: MORTON DEUTSCH AND ROBERT M. KRAUSS: *Theories in Social Psychology*. New York: Basic Books, Inc., 1965.

7. GLENN M. VERNON: *Human Interaction*, 1965.

8. GLENN M. VERNON: *Human Interaction*, 1965.

9. ARNOLD M. ROSE: "A Systematic Summary of Symbolic Interaction Theory" in *Human Behavior and Social Processes*. Boston: Houghton Mifflin Co., 1962.

10. GEORGE H. MEAD: *Mind, Self, and Society*. Chicago: The University of Chicago Press, 1934.

11. ALFRED R. LINDESMITH AND ANSELM L. STRAUSS: *Social Psychology*, ed. 3, copyright 1968, pp. 233-234. Material reprinted by permission of Holt, Rinehart, and Winston, Inc., New York, New York.

12. HERBERT BLUMER: "Society as Symbolic Interaction" in *Human Behavior and Social Processes*. Arnold M. Rose (ed.). Boston: Houghton Mifflin Co., 1962, pp. 179-192.

13. ALFRED R. LINDESMITH AND ANSELM L. STRAUSS: *Social Psychology*, 1968, pp. 238-239. By permission.

14. ALFRED R. LINDESMITH AND ANSELM L. STRAUSS: *Social Psychology*, 1968, p. 236. By permission.

15. GLENN M. VERNON: *The Sociology of Religion*. New York: McGraw-Hill Book Co., 1962, pp. 27-34.

16. The use of the term "symbol" refers to the category of conventional "signs" outlined in other literature. See, for example, LINDESMITH AND STRAUSS: *Social Psychology*, 1968, and VERNON: *Human Interaction*, 1965.

17. G. A. MILLER: *Language and Communication*, copyright 1951, pp. 4-5. Material reprinted by permission of McGraw-Hill Book Co., New York, New York.

18. GEORGE H. MEAD: *Mind, Self, and Society*, 1934.

19. C. H. COOLEY: *Human Nature and the Social Order*. New York: Charles Scribners, 1922; ERVING GOFFMAN: *The Presentation of Self in Everyday Life*. New York: Doubleday, 1959; *Behavior in Public Places*, New York: The Free Press, 1963; *Stigma: Notes on the Nature of Spoiled Identity*, Englewood Cliffs, Prentice-Hall, 1963; *Interaction Ritual*, New York: Doubleday, 1967; ORRIN E. KLAPP: *Collective Search for Identity*, New York: Holt, Rinehart, and Winston, 1969; C. GORDON AND K. GERGEN: *The Self in Social Interaction: Volume I*, New York: John Wiley & Sons, Inc., 1968; J. MANIS AND B. MELTZER: *Symbolic Interaction*, Boston: Allyn and Bacon, 1967; A. STRAUSS, *Mirrors and Masks*, Glencoe, Ill.: The Free Press, 1959.

20. ERNST CASSIRER: *An Essay on Man*, Doubleday and Co. edition, pp. 42, 43, 44. Copyright 1944 by Yale University Press. Material reprinted by permission of Yale University Press, New Haven, Conn.

21. FRANCIS E. MERRILL: *Society and Culture: An Introduction to Sociology*, ed. 4, copyright 1969. Material reprinted by permission of Prentice-Hall, Inc., Englewood Cliffs, New Jersey.

22. GLENN M. VERNON: *Human Interaction*, 1965.

23. GLENN M. VERNON: *Human Interaction*, 1965, p. 81. By permission.

The fact of the matter is that for many Americans, government does not *seem* close to them. It is not a process in which they feel welcome. It is, instead, a distant often hostile system, making decisions for them, not with them. And for too many Americans, the response to this feeling is either to shun the public life, or else to disrupt it.[1]

SENATOR EDWARD M. KENNEDY

Every personality, and every social organization, is confronted at frequent intervals with the task of choosing among alternative desiderata. . . . Typically, such preferences are not random, but patterned. The patterns they exhibit are relatively stable. . . . This indicates that valuing (or preferring) is partly a function of socially acquired characteristics of valuers.[2]

WILLIAM R. CATTON, JR.

# 2

## VALUE DEFINITIONS AND
## PLANS OF ACTION

In this chapter we will introduce and discuss the concepts of (1) value definitions, and (2) plans of action associated with value definitions. Initially, our discussion will be focused on values and, therefore, a definition of the concept of value is needed (value is defined at this point in order to illustrate, through a later definition of value definition, the difference between the two concepts). Value is typically defined as *the learned meaning of relative worth of ends, objects, acts, and combinations of these.* "Relative worth" is understood to convey the notion of good-bad, pretty-ugly, expensive-inexpensive, and so forth. The key word contained in this definition of value is "learned." It is important because it alerts us to the fact that humans must learn the value of the objects, acts, ends, and so on. However, the definition is misleading insofar as it suggests that the value is a property of the referent. This definition of values informs us that ends, objects, acts, and so on can be valued; it further suggests that these things are values. It is our position that these objects are not values but, rather, have a value dimension imputed to them.

The newborn human being does not have an organized system of values which he can apply to the various objects with which he is confronted. Rather, he must learn which objects have what values attributed to them. If the objects were values and the value therefore inhered in the object itself (that is, if value were a *property* of the object and, therefore, not subject to human interpretation), then every individual would believe every object to have the same relative worth. Everyone would, for example, define the act of premarital sex as bad. The fact that all humans do not believe every object (or act, as in this example) to have the same relative worth (some individuals, for example, define the act of premarital sex as good) clearly illustrates that objects are valued, that is, value is attributed or imputed to the object in question. Specifically then, we are talking about *definitions* of relative worth, or value definitions. Thus, we can amend our definition of values to read as follows: *the learned definitions of relative worth attributed to ends, acts, objects, and combinations of these.* Our amended definition then refers to value definitions and not values. In this chapter we will extend our discussion of the connection between symbol and object to include this aspect of the process of symbolic labeling: the process of attaching definitions of relative worth to objects which enter into our interactions with others.

There is no inherent relationship either between a symbol and a value definition or between an object and a value definition. While the value dimension of a particular object is decided by man, it is conveyed by the symbol used to refer to the object in question. It is certain that we could not communicate concerning our preference (or lack of it) for an object if we could not utilize symbols. We could not, in other words, communicate about anything if we could not agree concerning the symbol to be used for representation. It should be clear, therefore, that the value definition of a given object is symbolically attached to it in the process of symbolic interaction. Like the object, the symbol which stands for it does not *have* the value definition—it conveys it, and the value definition conveyed by the symbol comes to be symbolically transferred to the object in the process of social discourse.

## SYMBOLIC NEUTRALITY

As indicated in the quotation of Catton at the beginning of this chapter, every individual is confronted many times during his life with the problem of choosing among desired ends, objects, acts, or combinations of these. An important question at this point is how these ends, acts, and so on, come to be defined differentially. We indicated before that humans communicate about these kinds of things through the use of symbols. Logically then, we must ask how the symbols which refer to various things come to have differential definitions of relative worth (symbolically, not physically). These definitions are not inherent; symbols are neutral until meaning is imputed to them.

## DEFINITIONS OF RELATIVE WORTH

Symbols have no inherent meaning. However, there are at least two ways in which meaning can be attributed to any given symbol or

20

combination of symbols. The first of these, which involves arriving at relative consensus as to what the symbol stands for, is different for symbols which refer to concrete things and symbols which stand for intangible things. It is important that the distinction is understood.

For symbols which refer to intangibles, meaning can be attributed by specifying the nature of the referent. By specifying the "thing" to which the symbol refers, the symbol is given a defined meaning. We can, for example, provide meaning for the symbol "God" by specifying the nature of the referent—God could be defined as an all powerful, all forgiving, transcendental being. The definition of God then becomes what the symbol "means," or its meaning. The symbol refers to a definition of God. On the other hand, the process of deciding the referent (not defining the referent) provides meaning for the symbol which stands for a concrete referent. In the case of the symbol "God" the referent is not available to the five senses and we come to "know" what it is only by our definition of it. For symbols with concrete referents the referent is empirical and the referent itself becomes part of the meaning. This is the first of the two ways in which meaning can be attributed to symbols —by *defining* the referent which is not available to one of the five senses, or *deciding* the concrete referent to which the symbol refers.

The second way in which meaning is attributed to symbols is in terms of definitions of relative worth. Definitions of relative worth are value definitions that go a step beyond the meaning of the first type and subscribe additional meaning to the symbol used to refer to any given referent. This process—attributing value definitions—is the same for both kinds of symbols. In the one case it is possible to subscribe the additional meaning to the symbol "God" that "God" is "good." And in the other case it is possible to attribute the additional meaning to the symbol "desk" that the desk is "beautiful." Thus, the additional meaning attributed to the symbol provides us with information as to the relative worth of the referent to which the symbol refers. The "goodness" of God and the "beauty" of the desk are examples of definitions of relative worth. Most symbols have meaning of relative worth in juxtaposition to other symbols. That is, the goodness of God has meaning in the context of the notion of the evil or badness of some other symbol, for example, Satan.

It should be understood that while it is extremely difficult to discuss symbols without making reference to corresponding referents, it is the symbol and not the referent that conveys definitions of relative worth. The process of attaching symbolic labels to referents is (as pointed out in Chapter 1) a completely arbitrary process. Any symbol or combination of symbols can be used to refer to any referent man chooses. It is true that the process of deciding (or defining) the referent for a symbol gives meaning to the symbol. However, the decision as to the relative worth of the referent is not to be found residing within the referent. Things become valued along a favorable-unfavorable continuum through a process of consensual agreement, and this agreement as to the relative worth of a referent is attributed to the symbol (s) used in making reference. Thus, definitions of relative worth, or value definitions, are communicated by the symbols used to refer to certain objects, not vice versa.

## CULTURAL CONNECTION BETWEEN SYMBOL
## AND REFERENT

It should be clear at this point that the process of establishing the connection between symbol and referent is a cultural process. What follows is a discussion of the connection between value definitions and referents: specifically, the cultural process through which symbols come to have a value dimension.

Man's symbolic behavior has as an antecedent condition the ability to reach some manner of consensus as to the meaning of the symbols he manipulates (Statement 3). Further, symbols may have two kinds of meaning. These are (1) meaning in terms of the referent itself or in terms of definitions of the referent, and (2) meaning in terms of definitions of relative worth of the symbol. The second kind of meaning involves value definitions.

Like symbols, referents have no inherent value dimension attached to them. That is, there is nothing inherent in the referent which dictates its worth, for example, its goodness, beauty, and so on. Deciding the relative worth of any given referent involves coming to a cultural decision about its value. Consensus as to the meaning (in value definitional terms) of a particular symbol is reached by decision as to the relative goodness, or beauty, for example, attributed to the symbol. The value definition attributed to the symbol is then symbolically transferred to the referent in the process of communication. In order to make this point clear, two quotations will be presented as illustrations. Writing on values, Curtis has stated:[3]

> Values are objects, ideas, or beliefs which are cherished. In America, such things as money and social position are valued highly, but we also have many values which are not economic; beauty is valued, as is art, music, and philosophical speculation.

In his comments on Curtis' work, Vernon makes clear the position we have taken thus far in this chapter:[4]

22

Some of the logical difficulties in defining goodness as a quality of the object rather than a way of defining the object can be seen in this (Curtis') quotation. It is first stated that values are objects, and then, in the next sentence it is said that "such things as money and social position are valued highly." These two sentences are mutually contradictory. The first indicates that the objects are values; the second that the objects are valued. These say quite different things. If the value inheres in the object, it is not at the same time a quality attributed to or imposed upon the object of the valuer. . . . Such confusion could be avoided if it were recognized that goodness (even though this is a noun) is not an empirical dimension of anything.

Value definitions are a cultural convention. Since goodness is not an empirical dimension of anything, it follows that differential value definitions come to be attributed or imputed to ends, acts, and objects through the consensus of man.

It is fairly obvious that the young child does not possess his own well organized system of value definitions. He must, of course, learn a system of values through interaction with others. Generally speaking, the individual comes to accept the system of values held by those people most immediately significant to him. Usually such people are the child's parents, older brothers and sisters, and other immediate relatives. As the child grows older he learns and emulates the value definitions of persons outside the family and those in social groups which have become important to him. Thus, human beings tend to share the value definitions of those who are important to them and, further, they tend to adopt the value definitions of those with whom they have had a satisfying relationship.[5]

At a later point in life the individual tends to disassociate the value definitions from the individuals from whom they were learned, and develops a belief in the value definitions in and of themselves. Brim and Wheeler have discussed this process as it relates to the development of the self, and their remarks are instructive at this point:[6]

The individual, when looking or acting toward himself as an object, must initially do so from the point of view of some significant other person. For several reasons, this view point becomes disassociated from any specific person, and the "I-me" component of the self thus is generated over time from a number of "they-me" relationships.
How would the situation develop in which the person is no longer able to recall or identify the other in the interpersonal relation,

that is, the other who was involved? It appears that both generalization and the inability to discriminate are sources of the "I-me" type
of relationship. The "I-me" relationship is the product of a body
of learning generalized from interaction with a number of reference
figures now nameless because their identity has been lost in countless
learning trials. . . .

Thus it is with value definitions. As the individual comes to take on
a system of value definitions as a result of "countless learning situations,"
he tends to disassociate his system of value definitions from specific individuals and view them as his own (exclusive) set of value definitions.
The individual may attempt to maintain "his" set of value definitions
even if, over time, they come to conflict with the originating individuals
due to the changing nature of their behavior.

We are now in a position to set forth additional statements concerning
symbolic interaction theory.

6. There is nothing inherent in any referent to which a symbol
   refers which dictates its goodness, beauty, and so on.

7. Consensus as to the meaning of a symbol is reached by agreeing
   upon the meaning to be attributed to the symbol.

8. Since human behavior involves symbol manipulation and consensus as to the manner in which symbols are to be manipulated,
   that is, what relative worth is to be attributed to a particular
   symbol, it involves value definitions.

9. The process of attributing value to any referent is a cultural
   process.

## VALUE DEFINITIONS AND PLANS OF ACTION

The quotation of Senator Kennedy at the beginning of this chapter
provides an excellent illustration of the process we will be discussing in
this section. Senator Kennedy attempts to illustrate how he views the
definition many Americans attach to government in this country by
stating that he sees many individuals defining American government
as hostile. The fact that many Americans define (in Kennedy's view)
their government as hostile is important in terms of value definitions. It
is, however, only one important factor to be considered from the perspective we have adopted in this chapter. Of equal importance is that
on the basis of this definition, Kennedy believes he is able to anticipate

the behavioral outcome of such a definition of American government. That is, because Senator Kennedy views many Americans as having a definition of government as hostile, he is able to anticipate, predict, or otherwise explain their behavior on the basis of knowledge of their definition, that is, they will, on the basis of their definition, either "shun public life of else disrupt it." This is the second important connection between symbol and referent that the symbolic process supplies.

Knowledge of the value definitions attached to symbols allows us to anticipate the actions of others in our interactions with them. We are able to anticipate these actions on the basis of the "plans of action" associated with value definitions. A value definition provides social meaning as to the relative worth of a referent; *plans of action provide information as to what actions should accompany the meaning of relative worth attached to a particular symbol or symbols.*

Consider the following value definitions which are relative to your position as a college student.

An "F" is a bad grade.

Cheating on an exam is wrong.

Hard study is good.

These three statements represent value definitions upon which the majority of students have reached consensus. In addition to supplying information as to the general value orientations of college students, however, the value statements also allow us to anticipate the behavior of students. Consider the following plans of action associated with the three value definitions listed above.

One should not make a grade of "F."

One should not cheat on an exam.

One should study hard.

If we are supplied knowledge of an individual's value definitions, we will be in a position to anticipate his behavior relative to the object, act, or ends he is defining. It is through this process—learning the value definitions and their associated plans of action—that individuals are able to anticipate the actions of others and, therefore, interact in a stable, consistent manner.

We are not contending that value definitions are static and once formed are not subject to change. Nothing is further from correct.

Value definitions, like all other aspects of human behavior, are constantly changing. It is obvious even to the most casual observer that systems of value definitions have undergone, and are undergoing, rapid change. The widespread approval of drug use among much of the population is an excellent example of the changing nature of value definitions. Further, the changing definitions of morality are evidenced in our dress, leisure activities, and topics of conversation. The important fact, however, is that although value definitions can and do change, they do not lose their usefulness to the symbolic interactionist. It very well may be that during the initial stage of change well organized plans of action are not available for changing value definitions; over time, however, new plans of action which are consistent with newly emerged value definitions are developed.

The plans of action associated with value definitions are called "norm definitions," and can be defined as a *general expectation that individuals will act or think in a defined way in certain situations*. A note of caution is in order here. Quite often norm definitions are discussed as *things* (the word "norm" is used as a noun). It should be understood, however, that norm definitions are not *things* but are exactly what the label implies, that is, definitions of expected behavior. Norm definitions then, are symbolic configurations and thus like all symbols are empirical and can be subjected to scientific investigation.

Norm definitions represent the system of expected behaviors of a society and serve to define social relationships in ongoing, everyday interaction situations, as well as in situations in which the interaction is considered to be more crucial for the social order than is everyday behavior. Once norm definitions become established, they tend to become regulative for subsequent generations. In other words, norm definitions come to be incorporated into the culture of a society as they endure over time. We will have more to say concerning norm definitions as a part of culture in Chapter 4. For the present, however, we will simply indicate that norm definitions are important to the social psychologist in terms of (1) the degree of importance people attach to a given norm definition, and (2) the severity of sanctions meted out to the individual who fails to conform to the expected behavior specified by the norm definition.[7] We do not intend to maintain, however, that there are norm definitions available for each and every situation with which the individual is confronted. Norm definitions are generally appropriate to those areas of human behavior in which society has at least a minimum stake. Thus, there are no norm definitions covering the order in which a person reads the newspaper, or whether he puts on his right or left shoe first. These kinds of decisions are left up to the prerogative of the individual and, therefore, norm definitions covering these situations have not been developed.

At this point we are ready for some additional statements concerning symbolic interaction theory.

10. In that symbols involve value definitions, they also imply plans of action, that is, what actions or appropriate behavior should accompany the meaning attached to a particular symbol or combination of symbols.

11. Plans of action are termed norm definitions.

## VALUE DEFINITIONS, PLANS OF ACTION, AND SOCIAL DEVIANCE

Chapter 1 asserted that if humans were unable to arrive at consensus as to the meaning of symbols, social interaction would not be possible. Further, we could neither understand nor anticipate our behavior. We have stated that no referent has any inherent quality to it and, therefore, the value dimension of a given referent is imputed arbitrarily. Ends, objects, acts, or combinations of these are not inherently good or bad. They take on these qualities to the extent that they are defined as one or the other through mutual consensus. Thus, the acts of premarital sex, murder, rape, theft, cheating on income tax returns, and so on, are bad only insofar as they are culturally defined as bad. Likewise, the ends or goals of prestige, wealth, security, education, and such are good only if they are defined as good.

There are numerous examples in the investigations of anthropologists which illustrate the point we are making here.[8] There are societies, for example, where premarital sex is not only condoned, but encouraged. Such behavior is considered "correct" in these societies. Further, in direct opposition to the system of marital monogamy which is defined as good in our society, there are several societies which practice polygyny as the accepted form of marriage. (Polygyny is a marriage of multiple mates wherein the husband has more than one wife.) In the United States, a person who has more than one marriage partner at a time would be accused of bigamy and punished under the laws of society only because bigamy is arbitrarily defined as wrong. The important point to be made here is that a person who is defined as a social deviant in one society could be behaving in a manner consistent with the prevailing values of another society.

Social deviance results when an individual or group of individuals does not adhere to the prevailing norm definitions. Norm definitions, it will be recalled, are general expectations that individuals will act or think in a defined way in certain situations. Accordingly, when the majority of society or of one's peer group has reached consensus as to value definitions and associated norm definitions, failure to act out the norm definitions or to hold the accepted set of values is frowned upon and differentially sanctioned according to the degree of relative consensus and the intensity with which prevailing values are held. This is no less true of the value definitions and plans of action which are an integral part of society's many cultural institutions. For example, religion is one institution that prescribes what is acceptable or unacceptable behavior for man in the secular world. Religion provides man with definitions of what is moral and immoral, what is good and bad, and what is righteous and unrighteous.[9] It enumerates, as Glock and Stark[10] have made clear, the religious responsibilities of the individual. According to Vernon:[11]

> Without biologically given drives or motivators to guide his interaction, man develops symbolic guides which he follows. He acquires definitions as to what he and others should do, and how they should relate themselves to each other. Approved patterns he calls good, fair, just, or moral. Disapproved patterns carry reverse labels. Man *learns* the moral system of his society and *learns* to have such a moral system. He learns to look for and to find a moral aspect of behavior. Once he accepts the premise that there is, in fact, a moral dimension, he is faced with the task of taking this dimension into account for the various aspects of living. Religious definitions are used by man to make moral sense out of his experience. [Italics supplied.]

Since religion provides moral definitions for man's behavior we should (on the basis of our previous discussions) expect to find religious definitions regarding acceptable and unacceptable, or moral and immoral behavior. We would expect, further, to find these reflected, at least to some degree, in man's actual behavior. As an illustration of behavior for which the religious institution provides value definitions and plans of action, consider the realm of man's sexual behavior—specifically, premarital sexual behavior. Religious institutions in the United States traditionally have opposed premarital sexual activity of any kind. As Reiss[12] has stated, "All of our major Protestant, Catholic, and Jewish groups condemn premarital copulation."

In a study of the relationship between religious commitment and premarital sexual permissiveness, Cardwell found that the more religiously devout individuals are more conservative in their sexual behavior. This study of New England college students concluded:[13]

> Now the fact that religion does influence self-definitions allows at least two possible ways of viewing oneself relative to religion: (1) one may be convinced that his behavior is in harmony with the behavioral standards set by religion, or (2) one may define himself as at variance with religious behavioral standards. The data which were collected for this study indicate that those individuals who have strong religious self-definitions also define themselves as in harmony with the behavioral standards religion has set forth relative to premarital sexual activity. For those who define themselves as at variance with religion, we would expect to find, based on our data, increasing permissiveness as regards premarital sexual activity. For those who define themselves as religious, engaging in premarital sexual activity would involve behavior which was incompatible with their self-definitions, and feelings such as guilt or anxiety might result. The price of resolving the guilt feelings may be too high a price to pay.

It is highly improbable that religion would be so viable in our society if it did not have consequences for the individual in the secular world. According to our definition, an individual who engages in premarital sexual activity would be violating value definitions held by the religious institution in our society and would, therefore, be classified as a deviant. Reiss, a sociologist who has devoted much of his scientific work to the study of human sexual behavior, suggested recently that premarital sex could, and should, be considered an act of social deviance. Reiss' position is consistent with the position taken here. Reiss maintains that while drugs, mental illness, and crime have been "key" areas of concern for those interested in social deviance, premarital sexual intercourse has not, in general, been included in this category of phenomena.[14] Stating that deviance has been simply defined as behavior "outside the community's tolerance limits," he is of the opinion that premarital coitus qualifies as an act of deviance.

Of the various approaches Reiss discusses, "labeling theory" comes closest to the perspective of the symbolic interactionist. As set forth by Lemert,[15] labeling theory makes a distinction between primary and secondary deviation. Primary deviation involves the everyday violation of norm definitions, whereas secondary deviations occur when the individual comes to think of himself as a deviant, and therefore, assumes the role of deviant. According to Reiss:[16]

Secondary deviance is, by definition, produced by societal reactions to deviant behavior, that is, by societal attempts at controlling deviance. This is the key proposition of labeling theory. When a deviant is labeled as such, his self conception may be affected so as to start him on what Becker (1963) calls "career" deviance. Deviance by this view is created by society; it results from the labeling of a deviant. Groups or "audiences" choose which to label as deviant, and then some of the particular individuals who are so labeled react and enter upon career deviation.

Thus, Reiss maintains that society has defined premarital sexual permissiveness as deviant, and therefore, the individual who engages in premarital sex is labeled as such. The process of labeling an act as deviant is directly linked to the prevailing value definitions in the society, cultural institution, or peer group to which the individual belongs.

It is important, however, to understand that the process of differentially valuing ends, objects, or acts, is not necessarily grounded in rational, individualistic considerations.[17] This is clear in a statement from Sir James Frazer's work, *The Golden Bough*.[18]

> Sacred groves were common among the ancient Germans, and tree-worship is hardly extinct amongst their descendants at the present day. How serious that worship was in former times may be gathered from the ferocious penalty appointed by the old German laws for such as dared to peel the bark of a standing tree. The culprit's navel was to be cut and nailed to the part of the tree which he had peeled, and he was driven round and round the tree till all his guts were wound about its trunk.

Of course, we would think such punishment excessive or, at best, undue. In fact, the probability that an individual would be punished for peeling the bark off a tree is extremely remote in contemporary American society, primarily because such an act would not represent a gross affront to the existing value definitions or moral order. Such an act did represent social deviance to the ancient Germans, however, because trees were highly valued and this value was deeply embedded in the moral order. Cuzzort has discussed the power of the moral order and its source:[19]

> The power of the moral order comes from the fact that it is a collectively held set of beliefs. That is to say, it is a set of strongly held beliefs shared in common by a large number of people—it lies

within the public as well as the individual domain. It is essential to understand that it is the collective nature of the moral order which gives it tremendous influence and which elevates it above any single individual. Indeed, the moral order acquires a solidarity *sui generis* (of its own kind). For this reason, crimes are more than an affront to the individual—they are a threat to the solidarity of the moral order, and the reaction is beyond anything which might seem reasonable to a dispassionate observer.

Emile Durkheim, an early French sociologist, addressed the possible sources of the value definitions which define a given act as "bad" and therefore an act of social deviance. According to Durkheim:[20]

> . . . we must not say that an action shocks the common conscience because it is criminal, but rather that it is criminal because it shocks the common conscience. We do not reprove it because it is a crime, but it is a crime because we reprove it.

Thus, any act can be defined as a deviant act because it is considered unusual or undesirable by society. What is important to keep in mind in view of our discussion, however, is that deviance is culturally, and therefore, symbolically, defined.

## COGNITIVE DISSONANCE

Leon Festinger[21] introduced the concept of "cognitive dissonance." Festinger's work is based on the notion that an individual tries "to establish internal harmony, consistency, or congruity among his opinions, attitudes, knowledge, and values. . . ." The individual's knowledge, opinions, and values are what Festinger labels "cognitive elements." As we have suggested throughout this chapter (and Chapter 1), knowledge, attitudes, and values are all symbolic things, and thus cognitive elements (as defined by Festinger) are incorporated in symbolic interaction theory.

According to the theory, pairs of cognitive elements can exist in any of three relationships: (1) irrelevant, (2) consonant, or (3) dissonant. As one might suspect, in the irrelevant relationship the cognitive elements in question bear no significant relationship to one another. In the second type of relationship, or consonance, one cognitive element follows from the other; and in the third, or dissonant relationship, the obverse or opposite of one element follows from another. That is, when we believe that one event will happen as a result of our belief and the opposite happens, we have what Festinger terms a dissonant relationship between cognitive elements. The event, in other words, does not logically follow from the belief. Inasmuch as the basic assumption of the theory holds that people attempt to maintain consonance among cognitive elements, we would expect pressure on the individual to reduce the cognitive imbalance created by dissonance. According to Festinger, there are three general ways in which dissonance may be resolved: (1) by changing one of the dissonant elements, (2) by adding new elements into the cognitive structure, or (3) by redefining the dissonant element as unimportant.

Consider the student who has accumulated an almost straight "A" average in college, and prior to graduation takes the Graduate Record Examination for entrance into graduate school. On the basis of his undergraduate academic average, the student expects to do quite well on the test. Suppose further that this above average student does very poorly on the test. In all probability, dissonance results for this individual. The dissonance can, according to the theory, be reduced or resolved by (1) changing his conception of himself as an above average student, thereby accounting for the poor performance; (2) claiming that the testing room was excessively noisy, hot, or that he had a terrible headache throughout the test and, therefore, his performance is understandable; or (3) redefining the test as an inadequate indicator of probable success in graduate school, and, therefore, unimportant. Likewise, when the professor who defines himself as an exciting, above average teacher with the ability to communicate difficult concepts with ease assigns failing grades to over half of his class, he may add a new element to his cognitive structure to reduce any dissonance created by the grades he assigned. He might, for example, define that particular class as composed of an unusually large number of slow or lazy students. Therefore, the grades are not a function of his teaching ability.

Thus, cognitive dissonance theory can be of some use in our analysis of value definitions and plans of action. It will be recalled from our earlier discussion that the learned definitions of relative worth carry with them general expectations that individuals will act or think in a defined way in certain situations. Cognitive dissonance may result when an individual or group of individuals adheres to a given value definition and is aware of the "correct" plan of action associated therewith, but acts in a manner contrary to the appropriate plan of action. For example, the student who cheats on an exam while holding a belief in the value definition that "cheating is bad" may have cognitive elements—in this case a value definition and an illogical plan of action—in dissonance with one another. He would, according to dissonance theory, make certain adjustments to resolve the dissonance. If the dissonance remains unresolved, identity and/or behavioral problems may arise.

A word of caution should be introduced at this point. It is possible, as suggested by some scholars, that the apparent tendency to reduce complex social situations to a single dissonance-consonance dimension is too simple to be credible.[22] Lindesmith and Strauss[23] provide an excellent elaboration on the difficulties of cognitive dissonance theory for the symbolic interactionist.

## SUMMARY

We have discussed value definitions and associated plans of action, and have indicated that neither symbols nor referents have an intrinsic value dimension. Symbols, however, come to have a value dimension attributed to them, and in turn, this value dimension is imputed to the referent.

We also stated that value definitions are learned by man in the process of socialization and, therefore, value definitions are cultural in origin. It was maintained that deviance can be understood in terms of failure to hold the dominant set of value definitions and/or failure to act in accordance with appropriate plans of action. In the event that value definitions and plans of action come together in an illogical configuration, cognitive dissonance may result. Thus, knowledge of the illogical configuration may make what appears to be unexplainable behavior make sense. We also presented additional statements concerning symbolic interaction theory, and they are presented below, along with those set forth in Chapter 1.

## CUMULATIVE THEORETICAL STATEMENTS

1. Human behavior is cultural in the majority of its aspects.

2. Human behavior which is identified as cultural is in response to symbols.

3. Humans are able to utilize symbols insofar as some consensus as to their meaning is reached.

4. Symbolic meaning is learned, that is, it is acquired through the process of socialization.

5. In the sense that human interaction is symbolic interaction, it is considered noninstinctive. By noninstinctive is meant that human manipulation of symbols is not regulated, or directed, by any biologic condition within the individual.

6. There is nothing inherent in any referent to which a symbol refers which dictates its goodness, beauty, and so on.

7. Consensus as to the meaning of a symbol is reached by agreeing upon the meaning to be attributed to the symbol.

8. Since human behavior involves symbol manipulation and consensus as to the manner in which symbols are to be manipulated, that is, what relative worth is to be attributed to a particular symbol, it involves value definitions.

9. The process of attributing value to any referent is a cultural process.

10. In that symbols involve value definitions, they also imply plans of action, that is, what actions or appropriate behavior should accompany the meaning attached to a particular symbol or combination of symbols.

11. Plans of action are termed norm definitions.

## NOTES AND REFERENCES

1. EDWARD M. KENNEDY: *Decisions for a Decade*, copyright 1968, p. 29. Material reprinted by permission of Doubleday & Co., Inc., Garden City, New York.

2. WILLIAM R. CATTON, JR.: "A Theory of Value" in *American Sociological Review* 24:310-311, No. 3, June, 1959. Material reprinted by permission of publisher.

3. JACK H. CURTIS: *Social Psychology*, copyright 1960, pp. 138-139. Material reprinted by permission of McGraw-Hill Book Co., New York, New York.

4. GLENN M. VERNON: *Human Interaction: An Introduction to Sociology*, copyright 1965, p. 102. Material reprinted by permission of Ronald Press, Inc., New York, New York.

5. For further discussion of this process, see GLENN M. VERNON: *Human Interaction*, 1965, pp. 105-107.

6. ORVILLE G. BRIM AND STANTON WHEELER: *Socialization After Childhood: Two Essays*, copyright 1966, pp. 13-14. Material reprinted by permission of John Wiley & Sons, Inc., New York, New York.

7. JAMES W. VANDER ZANDEN: *Sociology: A Systematic Approach*. New York: Ronald Press, Inc., 1965, Chapter 2.

8. General discussion of anthropological studies of various cultures can be found in an introduction to anthropology text; see, for example, E. A. HOEBEL: *Anthropology: The Study of Man*, ed. 3. New York: McGraw-Hill Book Co., 1966, Part 4.

9. GLENN M. VERNON: *The Sociology of Religion*. New York: McGraw-Hill Book Co., 1962.

10. CHARLES Y. GLOCK AND RODNEY STARK: *Religion and Society in Tension*. Chicago: Rand McNally & Co., 1965.

11. GLENN M. VERNON: *Human Interaction*, 1965, p. 362. By permission.

12. IRA L. REISS: *Premarital Sexual Standards in America*. Glencoe, Ill.: The Free Press, 1960, p. 162.

13. JERRY D. CARDWELL: "The Relationship Between Religious Commitment and Premarital Sexual Permissiveness: A Five Dimensional Analysis" in *Sociological Analysis* 30:72-80, No. 2, Summer, 1969. Material reprinted by permission of publisher.

14. IRA L. REISS: "Premarital Sex as Deviant Behavior: An Application of Current Approaches to Deviance" in *American Sociological Review* 35:78-87, No. 1, February, 1970.

15. EDWIN M. LEMERT: *Social Pathology: A Systematic Approach to the Theory of Sociopathic Behavior*. New York: McGraw-Hill Book Co., 1951.

16. IRA L. REISS: "Premarital Sex as Deviant Behavior," 1970, p. 79. By permission.

17. See for example, R. P. CUZZORT: *Humanity and Modern Sociological Thought*. New York: Holt, Rinehart & Winston, Inc., 1969, p. 38.

18. Quoted from R. P. CUZZORT: *Humanity and Modern Sociological Thought*, 1969, p. 38. By permission.

19. R. P. CUZZORT: *Humanity and Modern Sociological Thought*, 1969, p. 38. By permission.

20. EMILE DURKHEIM: *The Division of Labor in Society*, copyright 1960, p. 81. Material reprinted by permission of The Free Press, Glencoe, Ill.

21. LEON FESTINGER: *When Prophesy Fails*. New York: Harper Torchbooks, 1956.

22. N. P. CHAPANIS AND A. CHAPANIS: "Cognitive Dissonance: Five Years Later" in *Psychological Bulletin* 61:1-22, 1964.

23. ALFRED R. LINDESMITH AND ANSELM L. STRAUSS: *Social Psychology*, ed. 3. New York: Holt, Rinehart, and Winston, Inc., 1968, pp. 55-58.

In the garden of a country house, in plain view of passersby on the sidewalk outside, a bearded man can be observed dragging himself, crouching, round the meadow, in figures of eight, glancing constantly over his shoulder and quacking without interruption. This is how the ethnologist Konrad Lorenz describes his necessary behavior during one of his imprinting experiments with ducklings, after he had substituted himself for their mother. "I was congratulating myself," he writes, "on the obedience and exactitude with which my ducklings came waddling after me, when I suddenly looked up and saw the garden fence framed by a row of dead-white faces; a group of tourists was standing at the fence staring horrified in my direction." The ducklings were hidden in the tall grass, and all the tourists saw was totally unexplainable, indeed insane behavior.[1]

# 3

# DEFINITION
# OF THE SITUATION

In Chapters 1 and 2 we discussed symbols and referents and value definitions and plans of action as they relate to the interpretation of human behavior. There is another concept we will consider in this chapter, and our analysis of this new concept will have significant impact on the manner in which we view the previously discussed concepts, as well as their application in the context of human behavior. In this chapter we will devote our attention to the situation in which human behavior takes place. To suggest the direction our discussion will take, we will state that all human behavior is situation oriented—that is, human behavior takes place within the context of a given situation.

## GESTALT THEORISTS' VIEW OF THE SITUATION

By simply stating that human behavior is relative to the situation in which it occurs, there is a clear implication that there are "forces" or "properties" of the situation which act in a dynamic manner to affect interaction that occurs therein. Some social psychological theories come very close to this interpretation. Gestalt theory,[2] for example, characterizes the situation in which human behavior takes place as a dynamically active field, wherein "forces" are interacting with each other to determine, so to speak, the modes of behavior which are theoretically possible within the field. These "forces" or elements which occur within the "field" (situation) are analytically distinct on the one hand, but mutually interdependent (existing in a reciprocal relationship) on the other hand. As Lana[3] has indicated, "The behavioral environment is assumed to have the properties of a psychological field that is analogous to a physical field of force."

As constituent elements of the psychological field (situation), individuals are among the "forces" which operate to influence human behavior. It follows from this that human behavior inhering in a given situational context involves response patterns which are somewhat bound to the situation. Therefore, if we are to attempt to explain human behavior in a situational context, the specific cognitions of the interacting individuals *at that time*, as well as other properties or forces in the situation, must be known. From the perspective adopted in this book, however, it would be unwise to dwell on the interacting individuals and properties of the situation *only* at the time the situation is occurring. As we have emphasized throughout the first two chapters, we learn from other humans and what we learn is an important element which influences how we will perceive the situation and how we will act within it.

## SYMBOLIC INTERACTION AND THE DEFINITION OF THE SITUATION

Symbol learning (socialization) is a noninstinctive process. As human beings, we do not make some instinctual connection between symbol and referent. The connection that exists between these phenomena is *cultural* and, as a result, must be learned through the socialization process. Furthermore, we stated that social interaction is the process of two or more individuals taking each other into account. Since we learn from other humans (are socialized by other human beings), it follows that at least two individuals are involved in socialization. If we then define a social setting as evolving when two or more individuals take each other into account, it would also follow that symbol learning is acquired in a social setting. It seems clear that no two occurrences of two or more individuals taking each other into account (interacting) are exactly alike. From this view, we can state that no two interaction situations in which information is processed or imparted—even if the information is similar—are exactly alike. Furthermore, it would appear that this dissimilarity, however slight, affects to some extent the content (perception) of the information imparted. Thus, we can say that *all* occurrences of two or more individuals taking each other into account are situation oriented, that is, relative to the situation in which the interaction is occurring. We can see, therefore, the importance of considering the situational context of human behavior.

The symbolic interactionist takes a somewhat different approach to the interaction situation than does the Gestaltist. Situations are *not* defined as existing "out there in empirical reality." Nor are situations defined as possessing "forces" or "properties" which influence behavior and thus are an important element in human behavior. Rather, situations are constructed, so to speak, based on previous learning and experiences of the interacting individuals. To be sure, situations have certain physical properties that are present—chairs, lighting, physical layout, and so on—and these physical properties are important. However, these kinds of objects have meaning for social behavior only in terms of the definitions applied to them. There is no necessary one-to-one relationship between objects in the physical world and our definitions of them, and therefore, the meanings they have are grounded in the relative consensus of the human actors who define the objects. Our point here is that physical properties of situations are not "forces" which affect human behavior—rather, the *definitions* we have of the properties are important and, therefore, we respond to definitions of these elements rather than to the elements per se. In other words, behavior characteristically is not a direct response to environmental properties; rather, it consists of a succession of adjustments to interpretations of what is going on in the situation.

The individual categorizes the situation in which he is participating and attempts to arrive at a decision as to the role he should play and the appropriate behavior relative to that role. His perception of these factors may be more or less accurate based on his past experiences. If, on the one hand, the situation somewhat parallels past experiences in which interaction has proceeded smoothly, the individual's perception of the situation will in all probability be accurate. On the other hand, the situation may be of such a nature that past experiences may be of little value in arriving at an understanding of the situation. This latter case is probably characteristic of the problem encountered by the newly inducted soldier.* Every physical object or element actually present in the situation is not taken into account. Only those considered to be important and subsequently labeled as such are taken into account. Selective perception is involved. We will have more to say concerning selective perception later. Thus, the symbolic interactionist is concerned with the situation per se but, in addition, he also addresses the *definition of the situation* as a salient factor for human behavior relevant to a particular interaction sequence.

Defining the situation involves a process we shall identify as synthesization. Synthesizing (in terms of defining the situation) involves relat-

---

* Even here, however, prior socialization has an important role. Most males have played the game of "war" in their childhood and have, in effect, anticipated certain aspects of the role of soldier.

ing both physical attributes of the situation as well as organized experiences we bring into the situation. The organized experiences with which we will be concerned are value definitions and associated plans of action.

We have stated that we come to know what we know through socialization. It is for this reason, for example, that we are able to predict with a certain degree of accuracy that individuals who have not been socialized into the field of sociology will not have knowledge of the concept of the "looking-glass self."* What we are stating at this point, of course, is that knowledge is culturally defined.[4] Now if knowledge is culturally defined and situations are also culturally defined, it would follow that the accuracy of the definition of the situation for any particular individual is related to the concepts available to the individual as he defines the situation. In this sense, the process of defining the situation may involve seeing what one thinks *should* be there even though it is not actually present, as well as *not* seeing things (or interactions) that actually are there. The presence or absence of relevant concepts influences what one has been socialized to apprehend. *This process of seeing or not seeing certain things according to the concepts one has available to him is termed selective perception.* Selective perception then, is an important factor in the definition of the situation.

From the above discussion it is clear that the accuracy of the definition of the situation may vary from individual to individual in terms of the conceptional schemes he has learned. Thus, we can state that the definition of the situation is a reconstruction of past experiences, wherein the individual selects what he views as pertinent to the situation, synthesizes these factors and brings them to bear on the situation. This process depends, as we have stated, upon his organized perspective and, thus, upon the socialization process. In short, the individual categorizes the situation in which he is involved, locates himself within the situation, and on the basis of this, decides the appropriate role(s) to be played. As we have stated, this process depends, in part, on the conceptual schemes available to the individual.

One such conceptual scheme discussed is the organized system of value definitions and associated plans of action which have emerged from socialization. A value definition provides cultural meaning as to the relative worth of an object, whereas plans of action provide information as to what actions should accompany the meaning of relative worth attached to a particular symbol(s) (see page 26). The key word in the above statement is "should." The word "should" is important because situational factors usually have a qualifying effect on value definitions.[5]

---

* Socialization relative to the concept of the "looking-glass self" will be discussed in Chapter 5.

To be sure, the manner in which the individual synthesizes the relevant factors in a situation influences how closely he adheres to associated plans of action. For example, the individual may have been socialized to adhere to the value definition that profanity is bad and the plan of action associated therewith—if profanity is bad, one should not use profanity. Thus, for example, when we are in the presence of the minister or priest of our church the probability that we will use profanity is low. However, as the situation changes to, say, a gathering of fellow members of a college fraternity, the value definitions and plans of action may be modified and we may use profanity quite openly. Thus, value definitions and plans of action are relevant to the situation, as are definitions of relative worth and selective perception. Therefore situations usually have a qualifying effect upon the extent to which we adhere closely to our conceptual scheme of value definitions and plans of action. At this point we can summarize our discussion by introducing additional statements about symbolic interaction theory.

12. If symbol learning (socialization) is noninstinctive (see Statement 5), it follows that it is acquired in a social setting. An experienced social setting comes about when two or more individuals take each other into account.*

13. Any incidence of two or more individuals taking each other into account is situation oriented, that is, it is relative to the situation in which the interaction is occurring.

To this point we have stressed that the symbolic interactionist pays attention to (1) the situation per se, and (2) the definition of the situation. The remainder of this chapter will be concerned more specifically with the definition of the situation and factors which affect the manner in which we define the situation. We will direct our attention to (1) the individual who is defining the situation, (2) the other individuals present in the situation, either physically or symbolically, and (3) spatial and temporal factors as they affect the manner in which the situational elements are synthesized. Of course these are not exhaustive of possible factors which affect the definition of the situation. They are, however, the more salient factors and will, therefore, receive the majority of our attention. Failure to discuss other factors is not intended to minimize their importance.

---

* As we have indicated, there is often an important difference between an empirical setting per se and the experienced setting, which includes only the defined or recognized elements to which meaning is attributed or given. Statement 12 refers to the latter.

## THE INDIVIDUAL AND THE DEFINITION
## OF THE SITUATION

Of paramount importance in attempting to analyze the process we have identified as defining the situation is, of course, the individual who is doing the defining. The individual becomes human, as we have said, through the process of socialization. It is through early socialization experiences in the family that his initial encounters with situations take place. We would expect, in view of what we have stated in previous chapters, that these experiences will have a significant effect on the manner in which the individual defines situations he encounters in later life. As a young child, the individual becomes aware of the definitions of his family with respect to given situations. As he learns the common language from his family (including inflections and intonations of that language), he also comes to learn that certain moments of disgust, pleasure, and indifference occur repeatedly in similar situations. As our past discussions would indicate, these facts are incorporated into the individual's overall system of language, and he comes to bring them to bear in situations where he has characteristically observed them in use. Individuals who have younger brothers or sisters can easily recall instances when the younger child imitated their disgust or pleasure in a particular situation.

The point we are making here is that humans learn how a significant number of situations should be defined simply by being present in the familial context of ongoing interaction. We would expect, on the basis of this, that the definitions the young child acquires will substantially parallel those of the members of his immediate family. It is possible, of course, that as the individual grows older his definition of certain situations will disagree with those of his family. We will turn our attention to this problem momentarily. For now, however, suffice it to say that differing definitions of the situation have to do with the varying concepts available to the individual doing the defining. It should be clear, however, that the human has to *learn* how to define situations, and that this learning process begins in the family. Further, it is improbable that we ever completely eliminate all influences of family socialization with respect to the manner in which we define certain situations.

Since we have suggested repeatedly the importance of the socialization process, we might ask how individuals come to have definitions of situations which at variance with (are dissonant with) those definitions of the situation communicated in socialization. For example, we hear every day of the differences in definition resulting from a so-called "generation gap." Obviously then, differences in definitions of the situation do occur. We will not address the phenomena of the "generation gap" here, but will attempt to account for differing definitions of situations in terms of the range of concepts available to the individual.

Previously we stated that the accuracy of the definition of the situation is related to the concepts available to the one doing the defining. We may extend this idea further. Not only is accuracy relative to the concepts available to the individual, what we are capable of being aware of (so that we may in turn define it) is relative to the range of concepts which have been learned through past experiences. Due to the limited range of concepts available to the individual, we can state that those participating in any interaction situation will, in all probability, not be aware of all the factors involved therein.

An excellent example of the way in which concepts available to the individual influence the manner in which the situation is defined is the case of the nursing profession.[6] There is general agreement that the role of the student nurse contrasts drastically with her counterpart in the hospital situation. For example, Corwin and Taves[7] have suggested that nursing *students* are interested in meeting people and being of direct service to those who need help. Further, evidence based on the recruitment campaign of the nursing profession indicates that most nursing students conceptualize the situation in which the nurse works as one which defines the nurse as a "ministering angel" or "Florence Nightingale" and, evidently, they enter the nursing school program with this concept of the nurse. Here again, prior socialization is important. Students also appear to have these concepts reinforced throughout the process of socialization into the nursing occupation. Thus, on the basis of concepts available to them, *student* nurses define the situation relative to the *practicing* nurse as one wherein they can be of direct service to the people who are in need of help.

As Corwin and Taves have also suggested, however, once the student nurse enters the bureaucratic structure of the hospital and must answer to the authority of the floor supervisor or head nurse, her loyalty shifts from the patient to the hospital. Thus evidence indicates that the role conception of the student nurse changes once she begins to practice in a hospital setting.[8] In her study of work satisfaction among nurses, Maryo[9] gathered information which indicated that one of the primary areas of dissatisfaction identified by practicing nurses is the absence of a clear definition of nursing duties; they complained of being asked to perform tasks which conflicted with their conceptions of their duties. Further, Berkowitz and Berkowitz[10] found that practicing nurses were more apt to like best those patients who conform to their expectations

43

of an "ideal" patient. (The ideal patient in this case being the one who does not place a great deal of demand on the nurses' time, does not see himself as the most important patient in the hospital, and does not feel he is in constant need of treatment and/or medication.) Practicing nurses evidently have altered their definition of the situation in which they work from one which requires a "ministering angel" to one which defines the nurse as a representative of the hospital rather than the patient. The consensus is that this phenomenon indicates a shift in the definition of the situation for nurses. Thus, the evidence seems clear that the nurse *enters* the profession with one set of concepts and defines the role appropriately, that is, the nurse is a ministering angel. As she enters the bureaucratic structure of the hospital, however, new concepts are learned and the situation is redefined on the basis of these new concepts to be a contractual relationship between nurse and patient.

The individual, the one who is doing the defining, is of paramount importance in terms of definition of the situation. The human must *learn* to define the situation. Early definitions of the situation emerge out of the socialization process in the family. On the basis of this we would expect the individual's definitions of the situation to be somewhat parallel to those of his family. However, the definition of the situation at which any given individual arrives is somewhat relative to the concepts (which are acquired through experience) he has available (has learned) for use. Thus, in the sense that differing individuals have differing concepts available to them, we would expect the accuracy of the definition of the situation to vary from individual to individual. As new concepts become available to the individual (are learned), it is possible for new situations to emerge. This process was illustrated by discussing changes in definitions of the situation for nurses as they move from the student position to the position of practicing nurse.

Implicit in the above discussion of nurses (as we were discussing what was considered to be the "ideal" patient), is that behavior is directed toward others in the situation. As the student nurse assumes the position of practicing nurse, the importance of given individuals changes—those in the bureaucracy typically become more important. In terms of defining the situation, our concern will be on those other persons (others) present in the situation.

## THE OTHER AND THE DEFINITION OF THE SITUATION

Behavior relative to a situation typically is directed toward those other individuals present, either physically or symbolically, in the situation. If we can make an analogy to the theatrical stage, the individuals with

44

whom one person is interacting constitute the audience to which his behavior is directed. Retracing our steps through Chapters 1 and 2, human beings come to interact in a stable manner through relative consensus as to (1) the symbols to be used in interaction and what they stand for; (2) value definitions; and (3) plans of action. Humans not only learn these concepts but also come to expect, based on experience, that other people will *share* the meaning they hold for the concepts. Through knowledge that the others present in the situation will share our definitions, we are able to anticipate the kinds of interaction that will proceed in the situation, and how we should act toward the others present.

Typically, when we enter an interaction situation in which new acquaintances are present, we attempt to gain as much information about them as possible so that we may tailor our behavior appropriately. This, of course, will have significant influence on the manner in which we define the situation. As Goffman has aptly stated:[11]

> When an individual enters the presence of others, they commonly seek to acquire information about him or to bring into play information about him already possessed. They will be interested in his general socio-economic status, his conception of self, his attitude toward them, his competence, his trustworthiness, etc. Although some of this information seems to be sought almost as an end in itself, there are usually quite practical reasons for acquiring it. *Information about the individual helps to define the situation, enabling others to know in advance what he will expect of them and what they may expect of him. Informed in these ways, the others will know how best to act in order to call forth a desired response to him.* [Italics supplied.]

That behavior is tailored to others present in the situation, and that these others are important in terms of the definition we have of the situation has been illustrated in a recent study by Cardwell.[12] In his study of religious commitment and premarital sexual permissiveness, Cardwell found that as the relationship between two partners changes, there is a corresponding change in the definition of permissible sexual behavior. In essence, this study indicated that as the definition of the partner changes (from new acquaintance to fiance), the level of permissible sexual activity, and thus the definition of the situation, also changes. In other words, the definition of the situation changes as the definition of the others involved therein change. As previously indicated, the others involved in the situation are elements of the empirical setting per se. They are also elements of the experienced setting which includes, as we have stated, the defined or recognized elements to which meaning is attributed. To the extent that an individual is differentially defined, and this differential definition is synthesized into the definition of the situation along with other elements, the definition of the situation changes. Furthermore, as the definition of the situation changes, the behavior appropriate to the situation also changes. Thus, when we find ourselves in a familiar situation, but with different people, our behavior and definition of the situation will change to the extent that the "new" people call forth different responses from us. We can now make an additional statement concerning symbolic interaction theory:

14. Three factors are of particular importance when considering the process of defining the situation. These factors are: (1) the individual, (2) the other (or the individual(s) with whom a given individual is interacting), and (3) the situation in which the interaction is occurring.

## SPATIAL AND TEMPORAL CHARACTERISTICS AND THE DEFINITION OF THE SITUATION

All human interaction situations are structured with respect to spatial and temporal characteristics. We hardly need elaborate on the notion that certain human activities are typically defined as being associated with well defined spatial structures. Some human activities require certain spatial structures for behavior to proceed in an optimum manner. Industrial sociologists have alerted us to this simple fact. (Most of us would take this "simple" fact as self evident. It was not too long ago, however, that this was not very "obvious" to many employers as judged by the spatial facilities actually made available for their employees.) Therefore, the spatial characteristics of a situation are significant for the individual in terms of his definition of the situation and the behavior appropriate to the situation. It would not occur to any of us, for example, to hold a noisy party in the reception room (or any room for that matter) of a funeral home.[13]

As Berger and Luckmann[14] point out, considerations of temporality are also important. In the United States time is usually a factor of prime consideration to interacting individuals. Our lives are ordered with respect to temporal considerations and most of our activities are organized around the order imposed by the time definitions being used. In all probability, your instructor has given you a timetable for reading certain chapters of this text. In order to accomplish the required reading within the available time, it is possible that you had to omit some activities you desired to participate in.

Further, time is a consideration insofar as the attainment of certain positions or statuses is concerned. You must, for example, spend a certain amount of time in the primary and secondary levels of education before you can gain admittance to the college or university levels of education. Furthermore, there are situations wherein time definitions are a crucial factor—such as taking a final examination in college or competing in an athletic event. There are, in addition, circumstances under which time becomes increasingly important as the circumstances endure. The case of the combat foot soldier in Vietnam is an excellent example of this aspect of the temporality of situations. The longer he is in the combat zone the closer the soldier approaches the time to leave the combat zone. When he reaches the point that he has very little time left before being rotated back to the United States, time becomes of great significance in terms of the kinds of combat exposure the individual is willing to risk.[15] Thus, the temporality of the situation is a salient variable for the definition of the situation. Beyond these readily apparent considerations, however, time is of great importance for our definition of the situation. Even our leisure time—for example, the vacation—is used within limits imposed by the length of the time available. Thus, the vacation time available influences, at least in part, the situation in which leisure activity can take place. Both spatial and temporal considerations are important, therefore, in the definition of the situation.

## SUMMARY

Definitions of the situation do not exist "out there in empirical reality" but are constructed, so to speak, through the process of synthesization on the part of the individuals interacting in the situation. Synthesization, and thus defining the situation, is a learned process. Defining the situation is a process and continues throughout the duration of the interaction situation as new experiences, concepts, individuals, or spatial and temporal factors become known or learned by the individual.

## CUMULATIVE THEORETICAL STATEMENTS

1. Human behavior is cultural in the majority of its aspects.

2. Human behavior which is identified as cultural is in response to symbols.

3. Humans are able to utilize symbols insofar as some consensus as to their meaning is reached.

4. Symbolic meaning is learned, that is, it is acquired through the process of socialization.

5. In the sense that human interaction is symbolic interaction, it is considered noninstinctive. By noninstinctive is meant that human manipulation of symbols is not regulated or directed by any biologic condition within the individual.

6. There is nothing inherent in any referent to which a symbol refers which dictates its goodness, beauty, and so on.

7. Consensus as to the meaning of a symbol is reached by agreeing upon the meaning to be attributed to the symbol.

8. Since human behavior involves symbol manipulation and consensus as to the manner in which symbols are to be manipulated, that is, what relative worth is to be attributed to a particular symbol, it involves value definitions.

9. The process of attributing value to any referent is a cultural process.

10. In that symbols involve value definitions, they also imply plans of action, that is, what actions or appropriate behavior should accompany the meaning attached to a particular symbol or combination of symbols.

11. Plans of action are termed norm definitions.

12. If symbol learning (socialization) is noninstinctive (see Statement 5), it follows that it is acquired in a social setting. A social setting comes about when two or more individuals take each other into account.

13. All incidences of two or more individuals taking each other into account are situation oriented, that is, they are relative to the situation in which the interaction is occurring.

14. Three factors are of particular importance when considering the process of defining the situation. These factors are: (1) the individual, (2) the other (or the individual (s) with whom a given individual is interacting), and (3) the situation in which the interaction is occurring.

15. Inasmuch as human behavior is situation oriented, it is also "spatially" and "temporally" oriented, that is, individuals take each other into account in terms of the spatial and temporal characteristics associated with the situation.

## NOTES AND REFERENCES

1. PAUL WATZLAWICK, ET AL.: *Pragmatics of Human Communication*, copyright 1967, p. 20. Material reprinted by permission of W. W. Norton & Co., Inc., New York, New York.

2. For a thorough discussion of Gestalt theorists' views, see MORTON DEUTSCH AND ROBERT M. KRAUSS: *Theories in Social Psychology*. New York: Basic Books, Inc., 1965.

3. ROBERT E. LANA: *Assumptions of Social Psychology*. New York: Appleton-Century-Crofts, 1969, p. 79.

4. An in-depth discussion of the social base of knowledge can be found in PETER L. BERGER AND THOMAS LUCKMANN: *The Social Construction of Reality*. Garden City, New York: Doubleday & Co., Inc., Anchor Books, 1966.

5. See GLENN M. VERNON: *Human Interaction: An Introduction to Sociology*. New York: Ronald Press, Inc., 1965, Chapter 11.

6. JERRY D. CARDWELL: "Nurse-Patient Role Conceptions of Student and Practicing Nurses: A Typological Research Design." Paper presented to the Maine Sociological Association, Portland, Maine, 1968.

7. RONALD G. CORWIN AND MARVIN J. TAVES: "Nursing and Other Health Professions" in *Handbook of Medical Sociology*, Freeman, Levine, and Reeder (eds.). Englewood Cliffs, New Jersey: Prentice-Hall, Inc., 1963.

8. JERRY D. CARDWELL: "Nurse-Patient Role Conceptions," 1968.

9. JOANN S. MARYO AND J. J. LASKY: "A Work Satisfaction Survey Among Nurses" in *American Journal of Nursing* 59:501-503, April, 1959.

10. J. E. BERKOWITZ AND N. H. BERKOWITZ: "Nursing Education and Role Conception" in *Nursing Research* 9:218-219, Fall, 1960.

11. ERVING GOFFMAN: *The Presentation of Self in Everyday Life*, copyright 1959, p. 1. Material reprinted by permission of Doubleday & Co., Inc., Garden City, New York.

12. JERRY D. CARDWELL: "The Relationship Between Religious Commitment and Premarital Sexual Permissiveness: A Five Dimensional Analysis" in *Sociological Analysis* 30:72-80, No. 2, Summer, 1969.

13. GLENN M. VERNON: *The Sociology of Death*. New York: Ronald Press, Inc., 1970, especially Chapter 5.

14. PETER L. BERGER AND THOMAS LUCKMANN: *The Social Construction of Reality*, 1966, Chapter 1.

15. CHARLES MOSKOS, JR.: "Why Men Fight" in *Trans-action* 7:13-23, No. 1, November, 1969.

These ideals of the essential dignity of the individual human being, of the fundamental equality of all men, and of certain inalienable rights to freedom, justice, and a fair opportunity represent to the American people the essential meaning of the nation's early struggle for independence. In the clarity and intellectual boldness of the Enlightenment period these tenets were written into the Declaration of Independence, the Preamble of the Constitution, the Bill of Rights and into the constitutions of the several states. The Ideals of the American Creed have thus become the highest law of the land. The Supreme Court pays its reverence to these general principles when it declares what is constitutional and what is not. They have been elaborated upon by all national leaders, thinkers and statesmen. America has had, throughout its history, a continuous discussion of the principles and implications of democracy, a discussion which, in every epoch, measured by any standard, remained high, not only quantitatively but also qualitatively. The flow of learned treatises and popular tracts of the subject has not ebbed, nor is it likely to do so. In all wars, including the present one, the American Creed has been the ideological foundation of national morale.[1]

GUNNAR MYRDAL

# 4

# CULTURAL MATRIX
# OF HUMAN BEHAVIOR

Cultural behavior in the human animal is predicated on his ability to use and manipulate symbols in communication. The value definitions, plans of action, and definitions of the situation which are symbolically created by man set him apart from the lower animals. However, we have presented these phenomena (value definitions and so on) as separate aspects of the reality of man's existence as a cultural animal. But if this were so—if these phenomena were distinct—we would be unable to develop a social psychology of human behavior. We would, in other words, be making an appeal to these phenomena as distinct, unrelated explanatory attributes when confronted with changing behavior. What we need at this point is a unifying principle to synthesize the various phenomena which we have uncovered in our previous discussions. This unifying or synthesizing concept is termed *culture*, and it will constitute our focus of attention in this chapter.

Man's cultural behavior is predicated on his ability to use symbols in communication. Once symbols have their meaning established, however, the meaning has a tendency to evidence stability over generations and to be transmitted from one generation to another via the socialization process. The symbolic meanings which are handed down from one generation to the next (including value definitions, plans of action, and definitions of the situation) become accepted as "guides" for behavior in society. These "guides" provide both proscriptions and prescriptions for the behavior of members of society *as a collectivity* and, therefore, come to be independent of any particular member of society. The concept of "guides" for behavior will constitute the central topic of this chapter.

Chapter 3 emphasized that the definition of the situation involves a process termed synthesization. Anticipating the symbolic interactionist definition of culture, we will state that culture also involves the process of synthesization, albeit at a different level. Before considering the symbolic interactionist definition of culture, however, it will be well to examine the various ways in which the concept of culture has been defined by other sociologists.

## CULTURE DEFINED

Social scientists have long been interested in the concept of culture and, as we might suspect, many and varied definitions of culture have been set forth. We will examine several alternative definitions in order to illustrate the features of culture the definitions hold in common. The attributes will then be incorporated into our definition of culture.

1. Tylor supplied the classic definition of culture in 1871. According to Tylor, "Culture . . . is that complex whole which includes knowledge, belief, art, morals, law, custom, and any other capabilities and habits acquired by man as a member of society."[2]

2. Abrahamson has a somewhat different definition of culture. According to Abrahamson, ". . . many diverse groups are linked together by common ways of doing things; eating, dancing, counting, building, etc. These established means and the implements involved—like forks and bricks—define a *culture*." He goes on to say that "In every society there are distinctive ways of getting food and eating, dancing and singing, worshipping, exchanging gifts, and so on. In total, these ways of doing things, and the beliefs that support them, define a culture."[3]

3. Lundberg and his coworkers defined culture as "a system of socially acquired and socially transmitted standards of judgment, belief, and conduct, as well as the symbolic and material products of the resulting conventional patterns of behavior."[4]

4. Still another definition of culture has been offered by Nisbet. He states that "The concept of culture is indispensable to any understanding of human behavior. We think of culture as the aggregate or total of all the ways of behavior, feeling, thought, and judgment which are learned by man in society."[5]

The list of definitions of culture could go on and on, and we will add our own definition of culture a bit later. However, first we will examine the four definitions outlined above in an attempt to synthesize or integrate their common features.

According to Tylor culture is a "complex whole." This complex whole is composed of knowledge, belief, art, morals, law, custom, and any other capabilities and habits acquired by man as a member of society and, therefore, in a social setting. This is consistent with our previous discussions. Insofar as the elements of culture (the complex whole) are concerned, it is clear that Tylor intended for his definition to include those aspects of man's world which are symbolically defined. Furthermore, beliefs are widely held relative to the consensus of the human beings who hold them and are, as is knowledge, culturally defined. In addition, that which constitutes art, morals, law, and custom is a product of consensus.

As Tylor states, culture is composed of elements acquired by man as a member of society. Although not explicitly stated in the definition, it is implicitly suggested that these elements must be formed together (synthesized) into a meaningful "complex whole." In other words, the various elements are not haphazardly related to one another, but are synthesized into a complex whole which "makes sense" in terms of human behavior. To be consistent with our discussions in previous chapters, we can simply substitute the word *learned* for the word *acquired* in Tylor's definition without any loss of meaning for the definition. Thus, Tylor's definition informs us that culture (1) is a symbolic phenomenon, (2) is learned by man through socialization in society, and (3) is a synthesis (complex whole) of man's many symbolic definitions.

When we consider Abrahamson's definition, an element implicit in Tylor's definition becomes explicit. That is, the elements of the complex whole are obviously *shared* in that "many diverse groups are *linked* together by *common ways* of doing things. . . ." Obviously, for "common ways" to be "linked" to diverse groups, they must be *shared*, or held in common by those groups. According to Abrahamson, this definition includes implements as well as artifacts—"like forks and bricks"—which are the products of human technology. Also, the beliefs that support the ways of doing things are included in the definition of culture.

There is a crucial concept introduced in this definition of culture. Abrahamson includes the notion of "counting" as one of the common ways of doing things. Numbers, of course, are symbolic things. It is to the extent that humans can agree what the numbers represent that we can build bridges and buildings or design cars. Were humans unable to agree as to the meaning of simple number systems, that is, if people used idiosyncratic number systems, blueprints for such diverse things as houses and rockets would be utterly useless. The point here is that while implements and artifacts are certainly part of culture (as Abraham-son defines it), it is consensus as to the meaning of these things that is of particular importance. In summary, this definition alerts us to the following salient aspects of culture: (1) culture is shared, (2) culture is composed of beliefs, and (3) culture is a configuration of implements and artifacts, and their usefulness is consensually defined. (Notice that the notion of culture as learned is only implicit in this definition.)

The Lundberg definition of culture introduces two new insights. In addition to being socially acquired (learned), culture is socially trans-mitted (from generation to generation). Furthermore, "material prod-ucts" are viewed as important in terms of the manner in which they are results of "conventional patterns of behavior," and therefore, the results of man's *definitions* about what constitutes conventional behavior.

The Nisbet definition also views culture as composed of a configura-tion of elements (behavior, feeling, thought, and judgment). Culture is (1) learned in a social context, and (2) is the total of man's modes of behavior. (Material things are not included in this definition.)

Thus, while each has different features, these four definitions of cul-ture share certain characteristics, which can be listed as follows: (1) culture is a symbolic phenomenon and, therefore, is uniquely human; (2) culture is a configuration of man's definitions about behavior per se, and about behavior relative to material objects; (3) culture consists of a meaningful synthesis of this configuration of definitions; (4) cul-ture is shared by the members of the group (is the common property of the group); (5) culture is transmitted from one generation to the next and is cumulative; and (6) culture is learned. You may recognize that each of these elements of culture is grounded in symbolic processes. With this in mind, we will turn our discussion to the symbolic interac-tionist conception of culture.

## CULTURE FROM THE SYMBOLIC INTERACTIONIST PERSPECTIVE

Within the symbolic interactionist frame of reference, culture is a term used to denote the totality of man's symbolic heritage. It refers to what any given group of people would define as their "normal way of living." As we emphasized in Chapters 1 through 3, the neonate is not brought into the world as a functioning human being. Rather, he must learn the meanings of symbols and the appropriate referents through the process of socialization. Furthermore, he learns the prevalent value definitions and the associated plans of action, as well as how to define the situation. He must learn, in other words, the "normal way of living" shared by the group into which he is born. The society of which he is a member has established a complex set of definitions which provide guides for acceptable and unacceptable behavior, along with a corresponding set of sanctions or laws to deal with those individuals who violate the cultural guides.

Among the normative guides that the society provides for the infant are stipulations as to the language he will speak, the kinds of clothes he will wear, whether he will assume a masculine or feminine role, the kind and amount of food he will eat, the social class he will occupy initially, the location as well as the kind of school he will attend, the manner in which he will participate in choosing the government and when he will be eligible to vote, the sports in which he will participate, and the alphabet which he will use to communicate through writing. The list could, of course, go on and on. The main point to be grasped here, however, is that culture is, as Tylor states, a complex whole. From our perspective this complex whole is primarily composed of the varied definitions concerning accepted, or normal behavior that the members of a society hold as defining their way of life. Of course, culture does not refer only to normal behavior. Culture also refers to that behavior which is often labeled as abnormal or deviant behavior. This will become clear in our discussion of the Southerner, whose behavior deviates from the larger societal norms.

Although culture as we have defined it is extremely complex, the more salient factors can be set forth as follows:

1.  Culture is a symbolic phenomenon. Furthermore, because it is symbolic, it is a uniquely human phenomenon.

2.  Culture is learned. Cultural definitions are not inborn in the human infant but, rather, have been previously formulated by society and must be learned through socialization. Culture is a learned configuration of man's definitions about behavior that comprises acceptable behavior and the "normal way of living" in the group.

3.  Culture is cumulative. Since culture is learned through socialization, it is passed down from one generation to the next, with one cultural generation building upon the culture of the preceding generation.

4.  Culture is constantly changing. New individuals must be socialized into the group's common culture, and this culture changes to the extent that new ways of perceiving the transmitted cultural definitions are evolved. Culture is never completely static.

Generally speaking, the individual comes to take on his personal identity within the context of the culture that is transmitted to him through the socialization process. His personality, in the majority of its aspects, is not idiosyncratic, but is an expression of the manner in which the common culture is transmitted to him, as well as his own interpretation of that culture and its expectations for normative life. Personality, then, can be conceptualized as the individual's expression of the culture into which he has been socialized. In view of this phenomena, it is not very surprising that psychological anthropologists, cultural anthropologists, and others have launched massive investigations in an attempt to uncover the "modal" personality type of particular societies.* We will have more to say on this later.

The main point here is that human behavior occurs within a general configuration, or matrix, of definitions relative to what constitutes a group's "normal way of life," and that an understanding of the constitution of this matrix, or culture, is of central importance in making sense out of human behavior. What appears as utterly nonsensical behavior to a person from one culture may seem perfectly "normal" to a person from another culture. It depends on the manner in which the culture defines the "normal way of living."

## CULTURAL DEFINITIONS

Culture provides a general guide for what the members of a group consider their normal way of living. In an attempt to analyze and understand culture, we may conceive of the normal ways of living of a group as organized around a set of "core value definitions." "Core value definitions" are those value definitions which have a high priority or preference relative to other value definitions. As Lindgren has stated:[6]

> "Fair play" may be considered to be a core value in Anglo-American cultures, because a whole complex of attitudes and values is dependent on it—willingness to abide by referees' decisions even when they are disliked, the use of a light line in game fishing, and so forth.

The idea is that a central or core value definition has implications for other value definitions and, therefore, is of special importance in terms of guiding human behavior.

Personality, as we have defined it, is an expression of the culture in

---

* Modal personality type is derived from the statistic, the "mode." In statistical terminology, the mode is the term that occurs most frequently in a distribution of terms. Thus, the modal personality type is that type which occurs most frequently in any culture and best represents the "typical" personality of that culture.

which the individual is socialized. The principle aspects of the individual's personality can be conceived as centered around the core value definitions of his culture. In other words, since the individual's personality is an expression of his cultural socialization, and since certain value definitions are more central than are others, the personality of the individual is predominately an expression of these core value definitions. On this basis we would expect humans to endorse these core value definitions and to act them out in their everyday behavior. Such is usually, but not always, the case. Evidence seems to indicate that there are certain value definitions that are widely held as core value definitions and, apparently, incorporated into the individual's personality. This same research also indicates, however, that at least some of these widely held cultural guides for behavior are *not* acted out in everyday life.

Consider, for example, Myrdal's theory of an American Dilemma.[7] Myrdal asserted that Americans are beset by an ambivalence generated by (1) adherence to a set of general cultural value definitions called the "American Creed" and, (2) the failure to act out the plans of action associated with that creed. Thus, the theory of the American Dilemma is essentially as follows: On the one hand, Americans hold the Christian-democratic value definitions of the "American Creed" and, on the other, fail to act out these cultural value definitions in everyday behavior. If Myrdal's theory could be verified, it would lend support to the notion that there are "core cultural value definitions" and that while these aspects are incorporated into the individual's personality structure, the manner in which they are expressed via personality is relative to the individual's socialization process within his culture. Based on our knowledge of the attitudes of whites toward blacks in the southern United States, it is possible to hypothesize the existence of such an ambivalence or dilemma as postulated in Myrdal's theory. Empirical investigations have been conducted in the southern United States in an attempt to ascertain the extent to which Myrdal's theory is an accurate synopsis of the actual state of affairs.

In a recent study in one of the states of the deep South, Cardwell[8] conducted research into the existence of the American Dilemma as regards social interaction between whites and blacks. The study consisted of a sample of sixty people who resided in the corporate limits of an industrial metropolis. The questionnaire used in this study was the same as that developed and used by Westie in his study conducted outside of the South.[9] The questions were of two types: (1) questions concerned with general cultural value definitions (or core value definitions), and (2) questions concerned with specific application of these core value definitions in black-white interaction (or potential inter-

57

## TABLE 1.

| General Valuation Statement | Per Cent (n = 60) | Specific Valuation Statement | Per Cent (n = 60) | Discrepancy* |
|---|---|---|---|---|
| 1. Everyone in America should have equal opportunities to get ahead. | | 1. I would be willing to have a Negro as my supervisor in my place of work. | | |
| agree | 90.00 | agree | 31.67 | |
| undecided | 5.00 | undecided | 41.66 | 58.33 |
| disagree | 5.00 | disagree | 26.67 | |
| 2. All people should be treated as equal in the eyes of the law. | | 2. If I went on trial I would not mind having Negroes on the jury. | | |
| agree | 93.33 | agree | 70.00 | |
| undecided | 3.33 | undecided | 11.67 | 23.33 |
| disagree | 3.33 | disagree | 18.33 | |
| 3. People should help each other in time of need. | | 3. If a Negro's home burned down, I would be willing to take his family into my home for a night. | | |
| agree | 100.00 | agree | 16.67 | |
| undecided | 0.00 | undecided | 60.00 | 83.33 |
| disagree | 0.00 | disagree | 23.33 | |
| 4. Children should have equal educational opportunities. | | 4. I would not mind having Negro children attend the same school as my children go to. | | |
| agree | 96.67 | agree | 38.33 | |
| undecided | 0.00 | undecided | 41.67 | 58.34 |
| disagree | 3.33 | disagree | 20.00 | |
| 5. Everyone should have equal right to hold public office. | | 5. I believe that I would be willing to have a Negro represent me in the Congress of the U. S. | | |
| agree | 78.33 | agree | 35.00 | |
| undecided | 11.67 | undecided | 38.33 | 43.33 |
| disagree | 10.00 | disagree | 26.67 | |

| | agree / undecided / disagree | | discrepancy |
|---|---|---|---|

6. Each person should be judged according to his own individual worth.

| | agree | 95.00 |
| | undecided | 0.00 |
| | disagree | 5.00 |

7. I believe in the principle of brotherhood among men.

| | agree | 86.67 |
| | undecided | 8.33 |
| | disagree | 5.00 |

8. Public facilities should be equally available to everyone.

| | agree | 70.00 |
| | undecided | 15.00 |
| | disagree | 15.00 |

9. Under our democratic system people should be allowed to live where they please if they can afford it.

| | agree | 65.00 |
| | undecided | 15.00 |
| | disagree | 20.00 |

10. I believe that all public recreational facilities should be available to all people at all times.

| | agree | 43.33 |
| | undecided | 15.00 |
| | disagree | 41.67 |

6. I would not mind if my children were taught by a Negro school teacher.

| | agree | 28.33 | |
| | undecided | 23.33 | |
| | disagree | 48.33 | 66.67 |

7. I would be willing to invite Negroes to a dinner party in my home.

| | agree | 10.00 | |
| | undecided | 11.67 | |
| | disagree | 77.33 | 76.67 |

8. I would be willing to stay at a hotel that accommodates Negroes as well as whites.

| | agree | 50.00 | |
| | undecided | 11.67 | |
| | disagree | 38.33 | 20.00 |

9. I would be willing to have a Negro family live next door to me.

| | agree | 15.00 | |
| | undecided | 20.00 | |
| | disagree | 65.00 | 50.00 |

10. I don't think I would mind if Negro children were to swim in the same pool as my children.

| | agree | 11.67 | |
| | undecided | 13.33 | |
| | disagree | 75.00 | 31.66 |

\* Mean discrepancy score: $\bar{X}_D = 51.16$; $\bar{X}_e = 81.83$; $\bar{X}_e = 30.66$.

action) situations. Each individual was asked whether he or she agreed, disagreed, or was undecided with respect to a series of questions designed to tap various aspects of the American Creed. Each individual also was asked whether he or she would agree, disagree, or was undecided relative to a series of questions that applied the general value definition to a specific black-white interaction situation. A discrepancy score was computed by subtracting the per cent agreeing with the core value definitions from the per cent agreeing with the application of those value definitions in black-white interaction. Theoretically, the larger the discrepancy score, the greater would be the confirmation of Myrdal's thesis of the existence of an ambivalance on the part of these Americans. The results are presented in Table 1.

As is obvious from the results obtained in this study, there was general acceptance of the core value definitions which represented the "American Creed." This finding would tend to verify the idea of "core value definitions." However, the discrepancy between the expression of attachment to the American Creed and the willingness to apply the Creed in black-white interaction was great. We can conclude, therefore, that Myrdal's theory is partially verified. But a more crucial question must be answered in view of our discussion of culture. On the basis of these results, we might be tempted to state that personality is not an expression of cultural value definitions but is uniquely individual and primarily idiosyncratic. However, such an assumption would be ill-founded. We may account for these discrepancy scores in the Cardwell study by introducing a new concept. The discrepancy scores can be explained, at least partially, on the basis of the socialization process characteristic of the *subculture* of the South. The new concept is, of course, that of *subculture*.

A subculture is a learned configuration of definitions which broadly parallels the definitions of general culture of which it is a part, but which has distinctive or unique definitions that are different from, or at variance with, the definitions that comprise the general culture. Any group as large as a society can be subdivided into a configuration of smaller groups. We may, for example, distinguish groups in society along religious, racial, or educational lines. The major religious groups most certainly share in the general core value definitions of their common culture.[10] However, they also evidence differing definitions (or interpretations) that can be accounted for on the basis of the particular religious orientation of the group. For example, members of the Mormon Church subscribe to the "principle of brotherhood among men" on the general cultural level. At the same time, however, their religious orientation provides a distinct definition of the role of the Negro within the more narrow religious subculture.[11]

Returning to the study of black-white interaction in the South, it becomes apparent that we can account for the discrepancy scores on the basis of subcultural socialization. It seems clear that in many respects the southern United States fits our definition of a subculture. Southerners, like those from other areas of the country, are taught to believe in the American Creed in the abstract, and most residents of the deep South will attest to this fact. We would expect that the American Creed (as a core value definition) would serve as an organizing principle for behavior, and thus would be incorporated into the personality of individuals. Recalling our earlier discussion of cognitive dissonance theory, dissonance should (in theory) result for any individual who has incorporated the American Creed into his personality but who, for one reason or another (such as unique subcultural definitions of the role and place of the Negro in American Society), fails to evidence congruity between his belief in the American Creed and his actual behavior. It is probable that some Southerners will evidence dissonance as a result of the discrepancy between belief and behavior under these circumstances. But how are we to account for the individuals who do not suffer dissonance?

On the basis of our discussions of the definition of the situation, it is suggested that subcultural definitions which prescribe unique definitions of the situation for interaction between blacks and whites serve as the basis for reinterpreting the applicability of the American Creed, and thus resolve potential cognitive dissonance. Evidently, Southerners have maintained subcultural definitions of the "approved" relations between blacks and whites that supplement the definitions of the broader culture which are concerned with the relations between men. "Black" then becomes a distinctive subcategory of "men" or perhaps another category which distinguishes them from white men and, thus, carries with it different plans of action and so forth. In other words, the label justifies the behavior. Additional information relative to the socialization of Southerners could be given.[12] However, the point to be made here is that "culture is to society as personality is to the individual."[13] To the extent that different persons evidence differing expressions of the cultural definitions via their personality, it is possible to account for the differences at least to some extent on the basis of subcultural definitions.

Recalling our earlier discussion of norm definitions (see Chapter 2), we can illustrate the manner in which subcultural definitions account for differing expressions of cultural definitions via personality. We have defined culture as the totality of man's definitions as to what constitutes a group's "normal way of living." As we have also suggested, certain of these definitions are considered more important than others and, therefore, serve to organize other, less important, definitions. The more salient, or organizing definitions we have labeled "core value definitions." We can, therefore, conceive of definitions which define a group's normal way of living as ordered along a continuum from the most salient (core definitions) to those that are important, but to a lesser degree than core definitions. Such a conceptualization is represented in Figure 1.

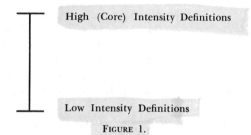

High (Core) Intensity Definitions

Low Intensity Definitions

FIGURE 1.

Core value definitions, as the most salient in any given culture, carry with them the expectation that the plans of action (norm definitions) associated therewith will be closely followed. Core value definitions are generally believed by members of society to be important to the welfare or continuing existence of the society. Violation of these value definitions usually results in severe negative sanctions for the offender from his group or society. We may take as an example the cultural definition which states that "honesty" should guide human behavior. The student who is caught cheating on a college examination usually receives rather severe negative sanction from the college community, for example, suspension or expulsion from the college or university. Core value definitions whose violation calls forth severe social sanction we will identify by the sociological term *core cultural definitions.*

At the other end of the continuum in Figure 1 are those definitions which are considered important, but to a lesser degree than core cultural definitions. Violation of these definitions usually does not result in severe negative sanction but in mild disapproval. Among these definitions would be such expectations as a college student should attend class regularly, a college student should make the highest possible grade, or a college student should dress appropriately for his role. Violations of these kinds of definitions usually do not call forth severe sanctions but are generally frowned upon by the members of the group. These kinds of definitions we will identify by the label *low intensity cultural definitions.* Thus, Figure 1 can be relabeled as shown in Figure 2. Value definitions can be conceptualized as falling along a continuum from high intensity definitions (core cultural definitions) to low intensity definitions (low intensity cultural definitions).

```
┬── Core Cultural Definitions
│
│
│
│
┴── Low Intensity Cultural Definitions
```
FIGURE 2.

Previously we stated that the American Creed represents one element in the general configuration of core value definitions. On the basis of the discussion developed above, we would expect individuals to follow closely the behavior specified by these definitions. However, we were not surprised when our examination of the application of these cultural definitions in specific circumstances (black-white interaction situations in the South) did not adhere closely to the specified norm definitions. The apparent discrepancy between the adherence to a given set of core definitions and the behavior associated therewith was explained, at least in part, through an analysis of subcultural definitions.

We may consider the specific application of core cultural definitions as falling along a continuum which illustrates how closely the associated behavior approximates the application called for by the cultural definitions. We will make use of the labels conforming and nonconforming to facilitate placing norm enactment along our continuum. If the application of a core cultural definition falls along the conforming end of the continuum, we will simply have reference to the notion that the core definition and its application are closely associated. In other words, conforming will be interpreted as meaning that the application of the core definition closely agrees with the norm definitions it specifies. The term nonconforming will, of course, be understood to indicate gradations of deviation from the specified norm definitions, with the far left pole representing extreme departure from the specified application. Figure 3 illustrates the continuum of application of norm definitions called for by core cultural definitions.

Nonconforming ├────────────────────┤ Conforming

FIGURE 3.

For an example of the manner in which these continua can be utilized, we will return to the study of the American Dilemma in the deep South. Consider the general valuation (core definition) represented by question three in Table 1. By examination of the response to that ques-

63

tion ("People should help each other in time of need"), we observe that all (100 per cent) of the people asked this question agreed with it. Further, it would seem reasonable in view of our previous definition that the notion that people should help each other in time of need is an American core value definition. Placing these responses on the continuum of cultural definitions yields a result as in Figure 4. This

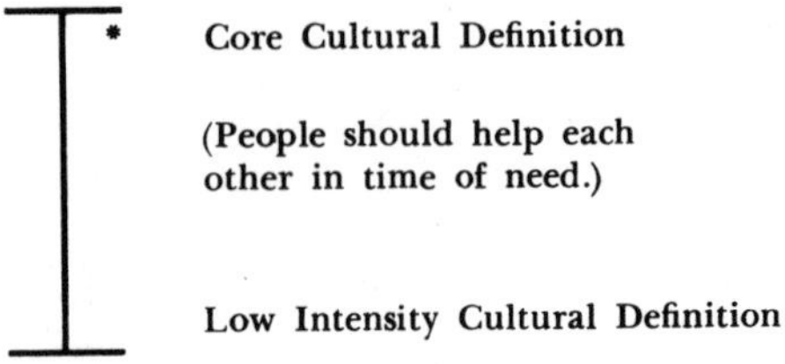

Core Cultural Definition

(People should help each other in time of need.)

Low Intensity Cultural Definition

FIGURE 4.

continuum clearly illustrates that this cultural definition is a core definition of high intensity. On the basis of the above continuum we would expect the conforming-nonconforming continuum of application of this cultural definition to fall close to the conforming pole. However, examination of question three as it applies to the specific valuation clearly illustrates that the discrepancy (as it applies to black-white situations) is quite large. Such a finding would suggest that any placement of norm enactment associated with the core cultural definition would fall near the nonconforming end of the continuum of application. Figure 5 represents the approximate point on the application continuum of the responses to the specific valuation statement ("If a Negro's home burned down, I would be willing to take his family into my home for a night").

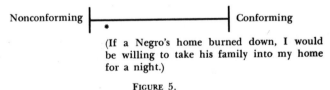

Nonconforming    Conforming

(If a Negro's home burned down, I would be willing to take his family into my home for a night.)

FIGURE 5.

The results in Figure 5 are not what we would have expected in view of the complete attachment to the core value definition. We can superimpose the application (norm enactment) continuum on the cultural definition continuum and obtain a more adequate indication of the magnitude of the deviation this study uncovered. This is done in Figure 6.

In Figure 6, the asterisk represents what we would expect to find based on the responses to the general valuation statement. The plus sign

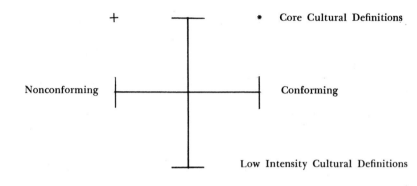

FIGURE 6.

represents an approximation to the actual state of affairs as represented by the responses to both the general core definition and its application with respect to black-white interaction. The discrepancy between the asterisk and the plus is quite large. What exactly does this mean; how can we account for the discrepancy? As we indicated earlier, the discrepancy may be explained on the basis of unique subcultural definitions of the South. While the people of the southern United States subscribe to the general valuation statement that "people should help each other in time of need," their subscription is tempered under certain circumstances because they also hold definitions which define the Negro as "different." By taking this fact into consideration, we might be in a position to account for (not justify) the discrepancy. In other words, the respondents might account for the discrepancy by stating that "helping each other in time of need refers to helping other whites," or "the government helps the Negro—no one helps the white man."[14] Theoretically, if the label "Negro's home" is replaced by the label "man's

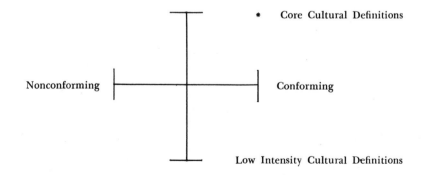

FIGURE 7.

home," the discrepancy would disappear (if, as we have maintained, the unique definition of the Negro is an influencing factor). Removal of references to the Negro in the specific valuation question might yield Figure 7. Thus, personality can be understood as an expression of general cultural definitions *as well as* specific subcultural definitions.

## CULTURE AND PERSONALITY

We have stated that culture is to society as personality is to the individual. In other words, the personality of the individual is relative to the general configuration of cultural definitions he has been taught. Fascinated by such a possibility, social scientists (primarily psychological and cultural anthropologists) have conducted large studies in an attempt to explore such a hypothesis. If culture were not an important element in personality, we would expect to find little or no evidence to the contrary in the various cultures of the world. We will now examine some of the evidence.

Ruth Benedict conducted one of the most famous and widely read analyses of primitive culture to date.[15] She studied and compared three separate cultures in a search for a distinct link between culture and personality. On the basis of her investigations, Benedict concluded that the cultural groups studied evidenced three distinct personality types which are listed below:

1. Zuni Indians of New Mexico: Evidence a strong belief in sobriety and moderation. Social interaction is deeply imbedded in ritual. *Apollonian* in character.

2. Kwakiutls of Vancouver Island: Evidence a strong belief in individual rivalry. Subject to paranoid delusions of grandeur. Significant emphasis placed on individual ecstasies. *Dionysian* in character.

3. Dobus of Melanesia: Generally treacherous. Life is viewed as a constant battle between the individual and the harsh environment. Characterized by a schizophrenic fear of nature and an unusually intense fear of their neighbors.

Benedict's classic study led her to conclude, in part:[16]

We have seen that any society selects some segment of the arc of possible human behavior, and in so far as it achieves integration its institutions tend to further the expression of its selected segment and to inhibit opposite expressions. But these opposite expressions are the congenial responses, nevertheless, of a certain proportion of the carriers of the culture. We have already discussed the reasons for believing that this selection is primarily cultural and not biological. We cannot, therefore, even on theoretical grounds imagine that all the congenial responses of all its people will be equally served by the institutions of any culture. To understand the behavior of the individual, it is not merely necessary to relate his personal life-history to his endowments, and to measure these against an arbitrarily selected normality. It is necessary also to relate his congenial responses to the behavior that is singled out in the institutions of his culture.

The vast proportion of all individuals who are born into any society always and whatever the idiosyncrasies of its institutions, assume, as we have seen, the behavior dictated by that society. This fact is always interpreted by the carriers of that culture as being due to the fact that their particular institutions reflect an ultimate and universal sanity. The actual reason is quite different. Most people are shaped to the form of their culture because of the enormous malleability of their original endowment. They are plastic to the moulding force of the society into which they are born. It does not matter whether, with the Northwest Coast, it requires delusions of self-reference, or with our own culture the amassing of possessions. In any case the great mass of individuals take quite readily the form that is presented to them.

In their study of the Russian modal personality, Inkeles[17] and his coworkers used a variety of projective techniques (Rorschach, TAT, sentence-completion) to ascertain the Russian modal personality. On the basis of these tests, the researchers were able to list eight areas of interest through which the Russian modal personality could be summarized. However, the investigators cautioned against the assumption that the sketch of the modal personality is "a simple and direct translation of particular test scores into personality traits."[18] The sketch of Russian modal personality characteristics is, rather, a summary statement based on the evaluation of conclusions relative to each test and on additional qualitative material. On the basis of these evaluations, the investigators sketched the Russian modal personality as centered around the following: (1) the central needs of the individual, (2) modes of impulse control, (3) typical polarities and dilemmas, (4) achieving and maintaining self esteem, (5) relation to authority, (6) mode of affective functioning, (7) modes of cognitive functioning, and (8) modes of conative functioning. According to Inkeles:[19]

To sum up, one of the most salient characteristics of the personality of our Russian subjects was their emotional aliveness and expressiveness. They felt their emotions keenly, and did not tend to disguise or to deny to themselves, nor to suppress their outward expression. . . . A second outstanding characteristic of the Russians was their strong need for intensive interaction with others, coupled with a strong and secure feeling of relatedness to them, high positive evaluation of such belongingness, and great capacity to enjoy such relationships. The image of the "good" authority was of a warm, nurturant, supportive figure. . . . Countering the image of the good authority, there was an expectation that those with power would in fact often be harsh, aloof, and authoritarian. This fits rather well with the finding that the main polarized issues or dilemmas were those of "trust vs. mistrust" in relations with others, "optimism vs. pessimism," and "activity vs. passivity," whereas the more typically American dilemma of "intimacy vs. isolation" was not a problem for many Russians.

Thus, Benedict and Inkeles would seem to agree with the statement that culture is to society as personality is to the individual. Of course other scholars have conducted studies into the impact of culture on personality. Honigmann[20] studied the Kaska Indians; Henry[21] examined Pilag Indian children; De Vos[22] investigated the Japanese; and Hus[23] the Chinese. The citations could, of course, go on and on. Our main point here, however, is that each of these scholars has agreed with Benedict in regard to the importance of culture as the shaping force of the personalities of the individuals in society. "No man is an island," and therefore, every man's personality is to some extent a product of his cultural socialization.

## CULTURE AS INDEPENDENT OF THE INDIVIDUAL

Culture is learned. The individual acquires culture from interaction with other humans. The group into which the individual is born possesses a common culture which is passed on to the neonate as he matures socially and maturates physically. If the newborn child dies at the age of seven days, the culture that would have been transmitted to him does not also die—it endures to be transmitted to the next human who enters the group. For the human who lives an average lifetime, the culture is likewise transmitted to him and it is possible that he will affect the culture imparted to him and will, therefore, change the culture. When he dies, however, the culture still endures. Perhaps it has changed somewhat, but it endures nevertheless. Culture is, therefore, independent of the individual.

Culture represents consensual definitions concerning the group's normal way of living, and because those definitions are based on social consensus they are *not* relative to any particular individual. They are relative to the group, and the death or disappearance of any particular individual does not, in turn, destroy the group's common culture. As long as the group endures its common culture also endures. It is possible, however, that after a group has ceased to exist its culture is taken over by another group and thus does not die.[24] Culture, then, is independent of the individual—it is a social phenomenon.

## CULTURE AND SELECTIVE PERCEPTION

In Chapter 3 we defined selective perception as the process of seeing or not seeing certain things according to the concepts one has available. Our discussion of culture suggested that the concepts available to the individual for use in his everday interaction are somewhat relative to the cultural setting into which he is born and, subsequently, into which he is socialized. Since perception is relative to the concepts available for use, two individuals from widely different cultures might selectively perceive the same situation in greatly different ways. It does not seem unreasonable to suggest that one or both of two such individuals may not be able to make any sense out of the situation. While the thesis of perception as relative to culture seems plausible, we can ask if there is evidence which would tend to support such a conclusion.

If we bear in mind that man is a symbolic animal and man's world comes to have meaning for him relative to the consensus as to the meaning of symbols used to represent his world, we can cite evidence which suggests the validity of the hypothesis of cultural selective perception. Language is, of course, the major symbolic system available to man for labeling his reality. The Sapir-Whorf hypothesis suggests, in general, that language serves as a guide to the "social reality of man." As Hertzler[25] has stated, "Language is not merely an incidental means of solving specific problems of communication and reflection; actually, the real world is to a large extent unconsciously built upon the language habits of the group. Each language represents a particular social reality." In an attempt to demonstrate the validity of the hypothesis of the importance of language in the world view (Weltanschauung) of man, Whorf conducted studies of North and South American Indian languages. On the basis of his analysis of these language systems, Whorf made clear his contention as follows:[26]

69

We dissect nature along lines laid down by our native languages. The categories and types that we isolate from the world of phenomena we do not find there because they stare every observer in the face; on the contrary, the world is presented in a kaleidoscopic flux of impressions which has to be organized by our minds—and this means largely by the linguistic systems in our minds. We cut nature up, organize it into concepts, and ascribe significances as we do, largely because we are parties to an agreement to organize it in this way—an agreement that holds throughout our speech community and is codified in the patterns of our language. The agreement is, of course, an implicit and unstated one, but its *terms are absolutely obligatory*; we cannot talk at all except by subscribing to the organization and classification of data which the agreement decrees.

We are thus introduced to a new principle of relativity, which holds that all observers are not led by the same physical evidence to the same picture of the universe, unless their linguistic backgrounds are similar, or can in some way be calibrated.

In terms of supporting evidence for the Whorf contention, suffice it to say that the data collected tend to substantiate the major contentions of the hypothesis. Language is, of course, an expression of the culture in which it is used as the means of communication. As to the importance of language as a means of selective perception, Hertzler has stated eloquently the point we are making here:[27]

Our given language, through the habits of identification and categorization which it develops in us, determines what we, the speakers, perceive in our environment—that is, what we notice, what we are conscious of, what is important to us, what can be ignored. We can perceive the objects, events, conditions of being and relationship of our experience only through types of knowns, as particularly represented by nouns, verbs and adjectives. The symbols *alert us* to what is for us "real," to what has existence and distinction of kind and detail among "things" and "actions," "states" and "qualities." These words function as spectacles for us, as we look out upon our world, and also as molds of and frameworks for comprehension.

As Hertzler goes on to say:[28]

A final aspect of language as culture index is that it reflects the essence of the culture of which it is both part and symbol so spe-

70

cifically that another language cannot serve as an adequate substitute. Many words and phrases of a language can be understood only by explaining them in their particular cultural setting. Similarly, many aspects of another culture cannot be expressed in a particular language because it does not have the words to do so.

Thus, it seems clear that the manner in which the individual will perceive his world and, therefore, the manner in which he will define acceptable and unacceptable behavior, involves selective perception. Further, the cultural setting in which the individual is socialized has significant impact on the avenues of expression his selective perception will take. Culture is indeed a synthesizing or unifying aspect of human behavior.

## SUMMARY

In summary of the discussion presented in this chapter, symbolic interaction Statement 16 is set forth.

16. The totality of man's norm definitions is termed his "culture." Inasmuch as definitions are learned through socialization, culture is learned. It follows that culture is social in nature and is independent of the individual, that is, it is learned and would remain even if a particular individual were not present to learn it.

## CUMULATIVE THEORETICAL STATEMENTS

1. Human behavior is cultural in the majority of its aspects.

2. Human behavior which is identified as cultural is in response to symbols.

3. Humans are able to utilize symbols insofar as some consensus as to their meaning is reached.

4. Symbolic meaning is learned, that is, it is acquired through the process of socialization.

5. In the sense that human interaction is symbolic interaction, it is considered noninstinctive. By noninstinctive is meant that human manipulation of symbols is not regulated or directed by any biologic condition within the individual.

6. There is nothing inherent in any referent to which a symbol refers which dictates its goodness, beauty, and so on.

7. Consensus as to the meaning of a symbol is reached by agreeing upon the meaning to be attributed to the symbol.

8. Since human behavior involves symbol manipulation and consensus as to the manner in which symbols are to be manipulated, that is, what relative worth is to be attributed to a particular symbol, it involves value definitions.

9. The process of attributing value to any referent is a cultural process.

10. In that symbols involve value definitions, they also imply plans of action, that is, what actions or appropriate behavior should accompany the meaning attached to a particular symbol or combination of symbols.

11. Plans of action are termed norm definitions.

12. If symbol learning (socialization) is noninstinctive (see Statement 5), it follows that it is acquired in a social setting. A social setting comes about when two or more individuals take each other into account.

13. All incidences of two or more individuals taking each other into account are situation oriented, that is, they are relative to the situation in which the interaction is occurring.

14. Three factors are of particular importance when considering the process of defining the situation. These factors are: (1) the individual, (2) the other (or the individual(s) with whom a given individual is interacting), and (3) the situation in which the interaction is occurring.

15. Inasmuch as human behavior is situation oriented, it is also "spatially" and "temporally" oriented, that is, individuals take each other into account in terms of the spatial and temporal characteristics associated with the situation.

16. The totality of man's norm definitions is termed his "culture." Inasmuch as definitions are learned through socialization, culture is learned. It follows that culture is social in nature, and is independent of the individual, that is, is learned and would remain even if a particular individual were not present to learn it.

# NOTES AND REFERENCES

1. GUNNAR MYRDAL: *An American Dilemma*, copyright 1944, pp. 4-5. Material reprinted by permission of Harper & Row Publishers, Inc., New York, New York.

2. E. B. TYLOR: *Primitive Culture*. London: John Murray Publishers, Ltd., 1871, p. 1.

3. MARK ABRAHAMSON: *Sociology*. New York: Van Nostrand Reinhold Co., Inc., 1969, pp. 8, 53.

4. GEORGE LUNDBERG, CLARENCE SCHRAG, OTTO LARSEN, AND WILLIAM CATTON, JR.: *Sociology*. New York: Harper & Row Publishers, 1968, p. 41.

5. ROBERT A. NISBET: *The Social Bond*. New York: Alfred A. Knopf, Inc., 1970, p. 223.

6. HENRY C. LINDGREN: *An Introduction to Social Psychology*, copyright 1969, p. 215. Material reprinted by permission of John Wiley & Sons, Inc., New York, New York.

7. GUNNAR MYRDAL: *An American Dilemma*, 1944.

8. JERRY D. CARDWELL: "The American Dilemma: A Southern Test," 1969. Unpublished paper.

9. FRANK R. WESTIE: "The American Dilemma: An Empirical Test" in *Race, Class, and Power*, Raymond Mack (ed.). New York: American Book Co., 1968, pp. 127-141.

10. GLENN M. VERNON: *Human Interaction: An Introduction to Sociology*. New York: Ronald Press, Inc., 1965, Chapter 6.

11. This information has grown out of conversations with members of the Mormon Church in Salt Lake City, Utah.

12. W. J. CASH: *The Mind of the South*. New York: Alfred A. Knopf, Inc., 1941.

13. GLENN M. VERNON: *Human Interaction*, 1965.

14. JERRY D. CARDWELL: "The American Dilemma: A Southern Test," 1969.

15. RUTH BENEDICT: *Patterns of Culture*. Boston: Houghton Mifflin Co., 1946.

16. RUTH BENEDICT: *Patterns of Culture*, copyright 1946, pp. 254-255. Material reprinted by permission of Houghton Mifflin Co., Boston.

17. ALEX INKELES, E. HANFMANN, AND H. BEIER: "Modal Personality and Adjustment to the Soviet Socio-Political System" in *Personalities and Cultures*, Robert Hunt (ed.), copyright 1967, pp. 312-339, Natural History Press, New York, New York.

18. ALEX INKELES, ET AL.: *Personalities and Cultures*, 1967, pp. 316-317.

19. ALEX INKELES, ET AL.: *Personalities and Cultures*, 1967, pp. 326-327. By permission.

20. JOHN HONIGMAN: "World View and Self-View of the Kaska Indians" in *Personalities and Cultures*, 1967, pp. 33-48.

21. JULES HENRY: "Some Cultural Determinants of Hostility in Pilaga Indian Children" in *American Journal of Orthopsychiatry* 10:111-122, 1940.

22. GEORGE DE VOS: "The Relation of Guilt Toward Parents to Achievement and Arranged Marriage Among the Japanese" in *Personalities and Cultures*, 1967, pp. 261-288.

23. F. L. K. HSU: "Family System and the Economy: China" in *Personalities and Cultures*, 1967, pp. 291-311.

24. GLENN M. VERNON: *Human Interaction*, 1965, Chapter 6.

25. JOYCE O. HERTZLER: *A Sociology of Language*. New York: Random House, Inc., 1965, p. 121.

26. BENJAMIN LEE WHORF: "Science and Linguistics" in *Technology Review* 42:229-231, 247-248, No. 6, April, 1940. Material reprinted by permission of publisher.

27. JOYCE O. HERTZLER: *A Sociology of Language*, 1965, p. 41. By permission.

28. JOYCE O. HERTZLER: *A Sociology of Language*, 1965, p. 106. By permission.

It is probably true that a man remains forever unknown to us and that there is in him something irreducible that escapes us. But *practically* I know men and recognize them by their behavior, by the totality of their deeds, by the consequences caused in life by their presence. Likewise, all those irrational feelings which offer no purchase to analysis. I can define them *practically*, appreciate them *practically*, by gathering together the sum of their consequences in the domain of the intelligence, by seizing and noting all their aspects, by outlining their universe. . . . It teaches that a man defines himself by his make-believe as well as by his sincere impulses. There is thus a lower key of feelings, inaccessible in the heart but partially disclosed by the acts they imply and the attitudes of mind they assume.[1]

ALBERT CAMUS

All the world's a stage,
And all the men and women merely players;
They have their exits and their entrances;
And one man in his time plays many parts. . . . [2]

WILLIAM SHAKESPEARE

# 5

## THE SELF AND ROLES

The concept of the self is of central importance in sociology and social psychology. While the self has been defined in various ways, our concern will center on what James,[3] Mead,[4] Cooley,[5] and others have identified as the "social self." The basic premise from which we will proceed maintains that the self is social in origin. Although this position is not universally adopted by social psychologists, it is consistent with our discussions in previous chapters. We will discuss *self definitions* (rather than the self), in an attempt to make clear the nature of the phenomena which concerns us and to avoid the possibility of reification of the concept. Accordingly, we will define self definition as *the set of all descriptions and concepts held by an individual for himself.* This description alerts us to the recognition that individuals do not have "selves" they carry around with them. Rather, people have ideas, or notions, about themselves which are the result of learning through interaction with others—in short, the result of socialization. The individual's self definition does not, however, represent the simple algebraic summation of interactions with others.[6] We will have more to say on this point later.

### BIOLOGIC BASIS OF SELF DEFINITIONS

There are certain biologic imperatives which impinge upon the individual and play an important part in the view he has of himself. We are referring, for example, to such biologic characteristics as sex, race, and mental condition—whether the individual is mentally normal or retarded. Clearly, under normal circumstances sex is a biologic trait over which the individual has absolutely no control. It is also a fact which he must take into account in his interactions with others. The same is true of race (a fact that is well documented for black Americans).

It is certain that the individual's experiences in social life do not determine his race. It is equally as certain that his race does influence the kinds of experiences he will have in society. In other words, social experience cannot be a cause of race, but an individual's race can be a cause of his experiences in society.* An individual is differentially evaluated and receives differential treatment on the basis of his race. There would seem, therefore, to be valid reason to assume that an individual who is aware that he is differentially evaluated would reflect the differential evaluation in his self definition. It is intuitively obvious that in predominantly white America, the black man's race is an important element in his self definition. While the importance of such biologic characteristics as sex and race is clear, we should keep in mind that there is often an important difference between a biologic condition, per se, and what the individual chooses to do about it.[7]

There are several biologic characteristics which must be present in order for the individual to acquire the ability to develop self awareness. These biologic conditions represent *necessary* conditions for the acquisition of a definition of self. However, they are not, in and of themselves, *sufficient* to insure the development of self definitions. This will become apparent as our discussion develops. Those biologic factors which represent necessary conditions are identical with those necessary to what we undertand as "humanness" in the physiologic sense. They are, in fact, those biologic factors which separate humans from the lower primates.†

Hoebel's sets forth the major morphological differences between the primates and other animals:[8]

1. Brain. Increasingly complex as one ascends the primate scale.

2. Eyes. Located well forward on the skull, rather than back and toward the sides. The back of the eye socket is closed and encircled with a bony ridge, whereas in other mammals it is open at the sides and rear. Vision is stereoscopic and very acute.

3. Face. Snout and jaws are reduced in size. Olfactory sense and dentitions are also reduced.

---

*There are individuals who have attempted to assume a particular racial identity in order to better understand problems generally associated with the racial identity assumed. While social experiences cannot cause race, presumably the individual's social experiences give rise to the desire to understand other racial identities. See, for example, John H. Griffin: *Black Like Me*. Boston: Houghton Mifflin Co., 1961.

† The biologic characteristics discussed herein are not to be confused with the racial biologic differences discussed in Chapter 1. The biologic properties discussed at this point are common to all hominoids.

4. **Hands.** (a) Forepaws are prehensile. The five-toed character-istic of primitive mammals is retained but the toes have a marked flexibility that makes extensive grasping possible. (b) Claws have become flat nails on top of the digits. (c) Digits have soft, fleshy pads on their undertips, richly provided with sensory nerves. Pri mates can feel and manipulate.

5. **Hind Paws.** Retain five flexible toes, while big toe is especially strengthened as a pincer. In hominids the foot is more clublike and acts as a weight-carrying base.

6. **Forearms.** Exhibit a high degree of flexion: that is with the elbow steady, they may be rotated clockwise or counterclockwise through almost a full circle.

7. **Reproductive Traits.** (a) Adults are sexually active the year around rather than only during well-defined rutting seasons. (b) Female normally bears only one offspring at a time instead of a litter. (c) Generally, the female has but two mammary glands. (d) Postnatal development is relatively much more prolonged.

Hoebel's goes on to say that:[9]

> Man, as the most highly developed primate, possesses all the above characteristics in their most clearly distinguishable forms. This means that he has by far the largest and most complex brain, eyes set fully forward in completely enclosed sockets with the back walls of the orbits fully formed, the smallest jaw relative to the brain-case, the fewest teeth, the most fully shrunken bony structure of the snout, the most flexion of the forelimbs, and the most upright posture of all primates.

The crucial biologic factor in man is the complexity of the brain, which enables him to think abstractly and express his abstract thinking via symbolic processes.

Even such factors as physical attributes (which are usually considered as biologically given) are differentially defined via symbolic processes. For example, in a recent study of the antecedents of self-esteem, Cooper-smith studied "a number of physical attributes that could conceivably be related to self-esteem."[10] According to Coopersmith:*

---

\* From *The Antecedents of Self-Esteem* by Stanley Coopersmith. W. H. Freeman and Company. Copyright © 1967, p. 120.

Some of these characteristics might confer enhancement by their very presence, such as beauty or height, and others might facilitate success in valued activities, such as strength and speed. Both kinds of characteristics are, to a large extent, beyond personal choice or control and both are generally assumed to have marked consequences upon self-esteem. It is, therefore, with some surprise that we found that the child's (present) physical attractiveness is unrelated to his self-esteem.

In view of the fact that this analysis was composed only of boys, Coopersmith suggests that physical attractiveness may not be "as salient a criterion of appraisal for the males in our culture as it is for females."[11] Such an interpretation is consistent with the position we have taken here—physical appearance may be biologically beyond our control; how we evaluate our appearance, and evidently, whether it is important to us, is not biologically determined. It is, as we have maintained, subject to the socialization process through which the individual progresses for its interpretation and importance to the individual.

Thus, man's biologic characteristics provide certain conditions which are necessary to the formation of self awareness. On the other hand, biology does not provide sufficient conditions for self awareness. In addition to the minimum biologic characteristics, man must be exposed to social experiences in order to acquire a definition of self. He can develop a self definition, in other words, only if he is exposed to socialization.

## SOCIAL BASIS OF SELF DEFINITIONS: THE SELF AS OBJECT

Humans acquire their definitions of self through experiences in the socialization process. The people, objects, ideas, and so on, which enter into socialization experiences are empirical and, subsequently, self definitions which emerge from these interactions are affected by these experiences. In addition to being empirically derived, self definitions have empirical consequences both for the individuals who hold them and for those with whom they interact. We will address this point in greater detail later. Presently, we will give further consideration to some additional factors in the analysis of self definitions.

We have defined self definitions as the set of all descriptions and concepts an individual has for himself. Explicit in this definition is the idea that the individual applies self definitions to himself. In other words, the individual takes himself as an object and applies labels to the object (himself). This process is particularly important for an understanding of self definitions (the process of taking the self as an object).

80

In other words, the human animal can take himself as an object and apply labels thereto in the same manner he applies labels to other physical objects. Thus, man can take his own body, his own beliefs, his own position in college, for example, as an object.[12]

The young child does not have a well established set of self definitions; references to himself as an object are centered on specific parts of the body.[13] Any extension to references other than the body are highly localized and usually centered on bodily movements. As the child matures and acquires the ability to think and communicate symbolically, he also comes to think abstractly and to exercise greater selectivity in discriminating relevant objects, acts, and experiences into his self definition.

It is difficult to state unequivocally when the individual has acquired a stable set of self definitions. We can assert, however, that once the individual has arrived at an established definition of the self it is relatively stable and resistant to change. We are not suggesting that self definitions never change—they do, but they are particularly resistant to far reaching modifications which would result in a major reorientation of the individual's perception of his nexus in the social structure. As Coopersmith has aptly stated:*

> Although the idea of the self is open to change and alteration, it appears to be relatively resistant to such changes. Once established it apparently provides a sense of personal continuity over space and time, and is defended against alteration, diminution, and insult.

As previously stated, once the individual acquires the ability to communicate symbolically, and thus to think abstractly, he is able to incorporate a wide variety of attributes of his environment into his definition of self. Is his self definition simply the sum of everything he incorporates into his own self conception, that is, are all factors incorporated equally important? If not, what are the factors which are considered important in terms of having the greatest impact on the individual's definition of himself? We now turn our attention to these questions.

## THE SIGNIFICANT AND GENERALIZED OTHER

Mead and Cooley have made significant contributions which provide important insights into these questions. Mead[14] alerted us to the fallacy

---

* From *The Antecedents of Self-Esteem* by Stanley Coopersmith. W. H. Freeman and Company. Copyright © 1967, p. 21.

of considering man to be an independent evaluative agent. According to Mead, every person knows himself primarily through the responses and reactions of other people to him. Man is, above all, a social animal, and his perceptions of others' feelings (attitudes) toward him exercise a profound influence upon the individual and are incorporated into his conception of self. Of course, not all persons are equally important to the individual and, therefore, we would assume certain people to play a more influential part in the formation of an individual's self definition. Such persons we typically label as "significant others." Thus, an individual's mother and father would usually be considered significant others, and we would expect them to play an important role in the pattern of self definitions the individual will develop. In a six-year longitudinal study of the self-esteem of children, Coopersmith evaluated the impact of parents as significant others on the child's definition of self. He concluded, in part, that:*

> The most general statement about the antecedents of self-esteem can be given in terms of three conditions; total or nearly total *acceptance* of the children by their parents, clearly defined and enforced *limits*, and the *respect* and latitude for individual action that exists within the defined limits. In effect, we can conclude that the parents of children with high self-esteem are concerned and attentive toward their children, that they structure the worlds of their children along lines they believe to be proper and appropriate, and they permit relatively great freedom within the structures they have established.

In the case of significant others, we can make the analogy, as did Mead, to the child's process of playing. As Mead points out, the play activity in which the child engages, "is a play at something."[15] That is, the child plays at being a mother, a father, a doctor, a policeman, and so on. He asks himself a question as a doctor and answers it as a patient. "He has a set of stimuli which call out in himself the sort of responses they call out in others. He makes this group of responses and organizes them into a certain whole. Such is the simplest form of being another to one's self."[16]

As the individual grows older and widens his world of human relationships, his self definition relates to a greater diversity of persons and social groups in which he has become a member. To state this another way, the individual acquires a wider audience, the reactions from which he

---

* From *The Antecedents of Self-Esteem* by Stanley Coopersmith. W. H. Freeman and Company. Copyright © 1967, p. 236.

also incorporates into his conception of self. This stage, the stage of the "generalized other," is qualitatively different from that of the "significant other." According to Mead:[17]

> . . . there are two general stages in the full development of the self. At the first of these stages, the individual's self is constituted simply by an organization of the particular attitudes of other individuals toward himself and toward one another in the specific social acts in which he participates with them. But at the second stage in the full development of the individual's self that self is constituted not only by an organization of these particular individual attitudes, but also by an organization of the social attitudes of the generalized other or the social group as a whole to which he belongs.

Sociologists and social psychologists have long been interested in various dimensions of the individual's self definition, for example, religious self definition, political self definition, academic self definition, and so on. Such concern with certain dimensions of self definitions alerts us to the consideration of at least two attributes of the individual's self conception: (1) self definition is multidimensional in content and, (2) there are several generalized others or social groups which contribute to the constitution of the individual's definition of self. The point we are making here is that people can be viewed as having only one generalized other to which they relate. According to Mead, "the attitude of the generalized other is the attitude of the community."[18] As we interpret this statement, Mead does not suggest that man has a single generalized other. Rather, the attitudes of the particular groups in which an individual holds membership are synthesized to form a larger configuration which embodies all of the groups in which he is a member. It is this configuration that Mead identifies as the "generalized other."

In the case of play, the child plays one role at a time. First he plays the role of the questioning doctor and next, the role of the responding patient. The pattern, however, becomes more complex as he enters social groups which are relatively enduring in time. In the social group he not only assumes his own role but must also be aware of the roles others are playing. He must anticipate not only his reactions to the other persons in the group but also their actions and reactions in order for interaction to proceed. This requires, of course, some ability to organize his perception of the roles of other persons in the group. As we have suggested, this process is a symbolic one. In the process of organization, these various roles are synthesized into the conception of self. According to Mead this process "represents the passage in the life of the child from taking the role of others in play to the organized part that is essential to self-consciousness in the full sense of the term."[19]

Thus far we have discussed the social basis of self definition in terms of (1) taking the self as an object; (2) the impact of the attitudes and reactions of others in self definition; and (3) the importance of the ability to anticipate the roles of others within the group. We emphasized that these three attributes are synthesized into a larger configuration which we have identified as the individual's self definition. What we have not discussed to this point is the process through which the individual evaluates the reactions of others toward himself. It is important to note that the development of self definitions is in part an evaluative process.

While many theorists of human behavior have concerned themselves with the evaluative process in the development of self definitions, Cooley[20] has set forth a conceptual framework which has received wide attention and general endorsement. We will, therefore, examine Cooley's thinking on the evaluative aspects of self definitions.

Cooley suggested that the attitudes and reactions of others are important to the individual's self definition in a "reflective" manner. The attitudes of others are reflected as though we are looking into a mirror and evaluating ourselves on the basis of what we observe. In the case of what Cooley termed the "looking-glass self," the others with whom we are interacting constitute the "mirror" from which we obtain the reflection. The idea of the looking-glass self embodies three essential elements: (1) the imagination of our appearance to the other person (s) ; (2) the imagination of his judgment of that appearance; and (3) some sort of self feeling such as pride or mortification. The evaluative dimension of self definitions is present in the last two of these three elements. As Cooley states, however, the concept of the looking-glass self does not, in and of itself, suggest the second element—although it is crucial in terms of the concept. Discussing the second factor Cooley states:[21]

> The thing that moves us to pride or shame is not the mere mechanical reflection of ourselves, but an *imputed* sentiment, the imagined effect of this reflection upon another's mind. [Italics supplied.]

Thus, "imputed sentiment" and "imagined effect" represent the process of evaluation on the part of the individual. Clearly, some sort of feeling such as pride or mortification involves evaluation of the responses of others. Further, it seems clear that continuous negative evaluation would have undesirable effects on the individual's self evaluation.

84

Thus, we would expect individuals to minimize the occurrence of negative evaluations resulting from interactions with others.

> This is evident from the fact that the character and weight of that other, in whose mind we see ourselves, makes all the difference with our feelings. We are ashamed to seem evasive in the presence of a straight-forward man, cowardly in the presence of a brave one, gross in the eyes of a refined one, and so on. We always imagine, and in imagining share, the judgments of the other mind. A man will boast to one person of an action—say some sharp transaction in trade—which he would be ashamed to own to another.[22]

In summary, only the human animal has the capability for self definition. As we have illustrated, this is primarily due to man's ability to take himself as an object and apply labels thereto. These labels are differently evaluated by the individual based on his perception of the reactions of others and their attitudes toward him.

## THE SELF AND THE SITUATION

As we observed in Chapter 3, human behavior is relevant to the situation in which it occurs. This is no less true for the individual's concept of self. The definitions that an individual has for himself develop within a given situational context. For example, the definition one has of himself relative to his ability at mathematics develops within the situational context of the classroom. If the individual performed poorly in math in grammar and high school classroom situations, the probability that he will choose math for his major college subject is diminished appreciably. Consistent with our previous discussion, we suggest that the individual's poor performance in math resulted in negative evaluation from others involved in the situation and these evaluations were incorporated into his definition of self. It seems reasonable to suggest that a student can define himself as unusually "bright" in most subject areas while holding a definition of self as below average in mathematics (we already have commented on the fact that the definition of self is multidimensional in nature). Accordingly, the individual who holds a definition of self as below average in math does not wish to place himself in a situation which he defines as one that would result in additional negative evaluations and he chooses to circumvent math entirely, if possible. We do not wish to labor a point to which we have already devoted an entire chapter. However, it is important to keep in mind that all human behavior is situation oriented and, therefore, so is the development of self definitions. Further, our reluctance to interact in situations which would tend to emphasize what we consider negative aspects of our definitions accounts, in part, for the kinds of situations in which we are willing to interact.

In summary of our discussion of self definition we may add two more theoretical statements:

17. Just as humans are capable of applying definitions to objects in the physical world, they are also capable of applying definitions to themselves. The totality of definitions the individual has of himself is termed his self concept or self definition.

18. Humans tend to behave in a manner compatible with their self definition.

## THE CONCEPT OF ROLE

Prior to a discussion of self definitions and the compatibility of roles, it will be well to turn our attention to an understanding of the concept of role. The quotation of Shakespeare at the beginning of this chapter supplies a vital clue as to the nature of the concept with which we are concerned. In fact, sociologists and social psychologists have adopted the concept of role from the theatre, and there are obvious parallels between the two uses of the term.[23] As Goffman has illustrated:[24]

The stage presents things that are make believe; presumably life presents things that are real and sometimes not well rehearsed. More important, perhaps, on the stage one player presents himself in the guise of a character to characters projected by other players; the audience constitutes a third party to the interaction—one that is essential and yet, if the stage performance were real, one that would not be there. In real life, the three parties are compressed into two; the part one individual plays is tailored to the parts played by others present, and yet these others also constitute the audience.

Thus, in effect we play many parts as human beings, and each of the parts has an associated role which must be learned in social life just as it must be learned and acted out on the stage. Consider your father. Obviously the role of father is one role he plays. During any given 24-hour period, however, he may also play the role(s) of (2) husband, (3) son, (4) sport fan, (5) grandfather, (6) engineer (or whatever his occupation happens to be), (7) or possibly night-school student. The list could go on and on. Quite obviously, the role of husband calls for different behavior than does the role of son, for example. Thus the expected behavior changes as the individual moves out of one role and into another. To make an obvious statement, we are not born with the knowledge necessary for acting out the many roles we will play; rather, we learn the appropriate "scripts" through socialization by others.

Generally speaking, the concept of role is the parent for three related concepts. Under the general conceptual heading of "role" are three additional concepts of importance to the social psychologist. They are (1) role playing, (2) role taking, and (3) role definition. We have already discussed role playing briefly, and we will have more to say about it later. Presently, however, attention will be directed to role definitions.

As before, we will begin our discussion with a definition of the phenomena which concerns us. Vernon[25] has set forth a definition of the concept which we will adopt for our purposes. Role definitions are defined as the *expected behavior patterns, or the plans of action which are associated with a particular position.* This definition informs us that role definitions (1) are associated with particular positions, and (2) refer to behavior that is expected of an individual, *not* to his actual behavior. Role definitions, then, are associated with a given position and entail the appropriate plans of action for playing the role for an individual who happens to occupy the position. It is important to recognize that role definitions are related to positions and not to individuals. For example, the role definitions which are associated with "combat foot soldier" remain the same regardless of who is drafted, or enlists, in the U. S. Army and subsequently enters the position. Failure to adhere to the role definitions of foot soldier, and thus to play the role outside *permissible* limits, results in the individual receiving disciplinary treatment. Thus, if the social psychologist has information concerning role definitions associated with a particular position, he will be able to anticipate the behavior of present and future occupants of that position.

Role definitions, of course, are not "naturally attached" to positions but are a product of human interaction. Humans decide what the role definitions for a given position will be and, subsequently, the young child learns the role definitions for any relevant positions through socialization. Some role definitions are spelled out in writing, as in the case of a job description in an industrial plant. Even the position of "college student" has certain role definitions formally set forth, such as dress rules, dorm hours, and rules regarding the consumption of alcoholic beverages on campus. There are, however, no written rules for some positions, such as boy friend or girl friend. The role definitions associated with these positions are learned through ongoing interaction. Nevertheless, we come to learn the expectations for behavior for these positions and learn what is unacceptable as well as acceptable behavior.

What is important for the social psychologist is that role definitions—including those not formally set forth—are widely agreed upon by the majority of society. An orderly society would not be possible otherwise.

Like all other aspects of human behavior, role definitions are subject to change and modification. The important factor, however, is that role definitions are associated with positions, not with individuals.

For the discussion of self definitions and the compatibility of role definitions, we will return to a consideration of the combat foot soldier. We have stated that an individual's self definition involves standards, descriptions, and concepts that the person holds for himself. We have also stated that these aspects of the individual's self definition have consequences in terms of behavior, that is, people tend to behave in a manner consistent with their self definition.[26] We would expect the individual to avoid those positions with role definitions that are incompatible with his self definition. An example of this avoidance behavior can be given in the person who views (defines) himself as a pacifist, and who receives an induction notice to serve in the armed forces. The role definition associated with the position of combat foot soldier may be incompatible (dissonant) with the individual's self definition and he may seek relief from service by claiming conscientious objection, or by leaving the country to avoid the draft. If the individual is drafted, however, once in the armed services he may apply for a position which would not require his acting out role definitions which were incompatible with his self definitions. Such an alternative may be occupying the position of medic. Our point here is not that people never enter positions whose role definitions are incompatible with their self definitions. They do—obviously not all soldiers are happy with the position they occupy. Some adaptation has taken place in order to minimize the incompatibility that exists. The point, however, is that there are circumstances under which behavior can be analyzed and interpreted as growing out of a dissonance between role definitions and self definitions.

## ROLE PLAYING

Previously, we stated that the sociological concept of role is closely related to the stage concept of role. Carrying the analogy somewhat further, we can state that role definitions are comparable to the "script" used by actors in playing their roles. Role playing, the concept we wish to consider at this time, involves acting out the "script" (role definitions) associated with a position. Just as the stage performer must interpret the script, so must the individual interpret the role definitions which guide his behavior. In this sense, all role playing involves dynamic, emergent, and creative behavior.

Consider for a moment that the individual must interpret the role definitions associated with the position he occupies. There are, pragmatically, several possible avenues the individual can take in terms of playing any given role. The initial task, of course, is to ascertain the definitions relevant to the role or associated with the position the individual is presently occupying. Upon identifying the associated role definition and satisfying himself that his interpretation of the role definitions is accurate, he may elect to play the role in a manner that is completely consistent with the role definitions. He may, on the other hand, make the judgment that the situational factors involved in the ongoing interaction are such that deviation or departure from the role definitions is appropriate, or at least permissible. Personal considerations may influence the individual's interpretation of the situation and play an important part in the decision to deviate from existing role definitions associated with any particular position.

Moskos[27] recently studied the American combat soldier in Vietnam in an attempt to understand "Why Men Fight." He provided an excellent example of the manner in which personal considerations may influence the decision to deviate from existing role definitions when playing the role of the "point man." The "point man" leads the combat squad on their patrols and is usually the first individual in the squad to contact the enemy. The army, of course, has formally set forth role definitions to guide the soldier in playing the role of the point man. According to Moskos, however, combat soldiers do not always play the role of "point man" in accordance with army regulations (role definitions) :[28]

> The point man is usually placed well in front of the main body, in the most exposed position. Soldiers naturally dread this danger-ous assignment, but a good point man is a safeguard for the entire patrol. What happens, as often as not, is that men on point behave in a noticeably careless manner in order to avoid being regularly assigned the job. At the same time, of course, the point man tries not to be so incautious as to put himself completely at the mercy of an encountered enemy force. In plain language, soldiers do not typically perform at their best when on point; personal safety over-rides group interest.

Thus, at least in the combat situation in Vietnam, personal considera-tions afford the individual an opportunity to reinterpret the situation, and provide a rationale for deviation and creativity in terms of playing the role of point man. As Moskos also points out, as the individual soldier becomes more experienced, his combat efficiency improves. However, the longer the soldier is in combat (and thus the closer he comes to having completed his tour), new interpretations of the manner in which the role should be played with regard to efficiency emerge:[29]

> Toward the ninth and tenth months, the soldier begins to regard himself as an "old soldier," and it is usually at this point that he is generally most effective in combat. As he approaches the end of his tour in Vietnam, however, he begins noticeably to withdraw his efficiency. He now becomes reluctant to engage in offensive combat operations; and increasingly, he hears and repeats stories of men killed the day they were to rotate back home.

Thus, role playing is emergent in that as the situation changes, role definitions are subject to reinterpretation and new ways of playing the role develop as old ways become unsatisfactory. Our main point in this section, however, is that role definitions are associated with positions, and *role playing involves acting out these role definitions.* In playing a role, the associated role definitions may or may not be closely followed. In situations wherein role playing does not closely follow or deviates from appropriate role definitions, role playing can be termed "creative." All role playing is somewhat emergent and dynamic.

## ROLE TAKING

Thus far we have discussed two of the concepts included under the general conceptual configuration defined as "role." To complete the analysis of role we will consider a third concept which we will identify as "role taking." Role taking is defined as *the process of interpreting the behavior of others.*[30] This definition alerts us to two important facets of the process of role taking. First, role taking is an evaluating process, and second, at least two individuals must be involved in the interpretative process (the evaluator and the evaluated).*

What do we mean when we state that role taking involves "interpretation of behavior"? In answering such a question, we should keep in mind that human behavior is essentially the acting out of role definitions

---

* As you will recall from our earlier discussion of the significant and generalized other, it is not necessary for the "other" to be physically present. We can relate to individuals—real or imagined—through symbolic processes, even though they are absent from the situation.

90

associated with a position and, therefore, we are concerned with interpreting the manner in which an individual or group of individuals is playing a role. Interpretation of role behavior often has been used synonymously with "understanding" and "empathy" and similar processes. Comparisons of such a type may be misleading, however, since they fail to denote the full import of role taking.

Role taking is an "intersubjective" phenomenon.[31] It (role taking) is intersubjective in the sense that an individual assumes the role of the other in an attempt to anticipate his actions and to evaluate how he (the individual taking the role) believes the other will react or respond to him. In role taking the individual incorporates not only how A thinks B will react, but also how he interprets the actual reaction when it occurs. As are all of the processes we have discussed throughout this text, the process of interpretation is a symbolic one. It is impossible, of course, for an individual to "get inside" of another and "know" what any particular individual is "really" thinking, or how he "really" intends to act in any given circumstance. If, however, it is impossible to "know" these kinds of things, we must ask the question of how we can possibly come to take the role of the other. We are supplied symbolic "clues" by the individual with whom we are interacting and whose role playing we are trying to interpret. These "clues" are, as we have maintained, symbolic. They may be in the form of facial expressions, clothing, intonation of speech, posture, or any combination of these and other factors.[32] Thus, the interpretation of behavior which allows us to take the role of the other does not involve "getting inside" the individual, but is manifested in the extent to which the symbolic clues the other supplies are understood (that is, shared) by the interpreting individual.

Consistent with the idea that interacting individuals or groups of individuals supply symbolic clues as to the manner in which a role is being played, we can state that the extent to which an individual shares (comprehends, understands) the symbolic clues being given defines the limit of effective or accurate, role taking.[33] We would not expect a person from the Bushman tribe of Australia to accurately interpret the role of a junior executive from New York, or vice versa. In other words, initial interaction between two such individuals would not be stable, but erratic. To put what we have stated another way, one of the conditions for accurate role taking is a "good fit" between the *symbols* presented and the *meaning* attached thereto by the interacting parties. This "goodness of fit" sets limits on the accuracy of the role taking process. Where the "fit" is good, the role taking process proceeds smoothly; where it is not, role taking may be erratic or inaccurate altogether.

91

At this point we may posit our final theoretical statements:

19. Since norm definitions are expectations for behavior (Statement 10), and since "scripts" (or expectations for behavior) are typical aspects of roles, norm definitions are characteristic of roles.

20. Because roles are characterized by norm definitions, it follows that they (roles) are an important part of man's cultural definitions.

Role taking, like role definitions and role playing, is an important dimension of the concept of role. The three are, of course, interrelated and one dimension informs us, to a certain extent, about the others. Each of these dimensions—role definitions, role playing, role taking— is important if human interaction is to proceed in an orderly, stable manner.

## SUMMARY

In this chapter we have discussed two important and interrelated concepts concerning human social behavior. These are the concepts of the self and of role. As we pointed out, each of the concepts has important subdimensions.

The human's ability to hold a definition of himself is not dependent upon biologic factors beyond the necessary condition of possessing them in their normal state. The acquisition of a definition of self is grounded in man's ability to take himself as an object and apply definitions thereto.

In terms of the concept of role, it is through knowledge of the "scripts" (role definitions) associated with positions that we are able to play a role in the socially accepted manner. Role taking provides for the anticipation of behavior of others and supplies the basis for continuing, stable interaction.

## CUMULATIVE THEORETICAL STATEMENTS

1. Human behavior is cultural in the majority of its aspects.

2. Human behavior which is identified as cultural is in response to symbols.

3. Humans are able to utilize symbols insofar as some consensus as to their meaning is reached.

4. Symbolic meaning is learned, that is, it is acquired through the process of socialization.

5. In the sense that human interaction is symbolic interaction, it is considered noninstinctive. By noninstinctive is meant that human manipulation of symbols is not regulated or directed by any biologic condition within the individual.

6. There is nothing inherent in any referent to which a symbol refers which dictates its goodness, beauty, and so on.

7. Consensus as to the meaning of a symbol is reached by agreeing upon the meaning to be attributed to the symbol.

8. Since human behavior involves symbol manipulation and consensus as to the manner in which symbols are to be manipulated, that is, what relative worth is to be attributed to a particular symbol, it involves value definitions.

9. The process of attributing value to any referent is a cultural process.

10. In that symbols involve value definitions, they also imply plans of action, that is, what actions or appropriate behavior should accompany the meaning attached to a particular symbol or combination of symbols.

11. Plans of action are termed norm definitions.

12. If symbol learning (socialization) is noninstinctive (see Statement 5), it follows that it is acquired in a social setting. A social setting comes about when two or more individuals take each other into account.

13. All incidences of two or more individuals taking each other into account are situation oriented, that is, they are relative to the situation in which the interaction is occurring.

14. Three factors are of particular importance when considering the process of defining the situation. These factors are: (1) the individual, (2) the other (or the individual(s) with whom a given individual is interacting), and (3) the situation in which the interaction is occurring.

15. Inasmuch as human behavior is situation oriented, it is also "spatially" and "temporally" oriented, that is, individuals take each other into account in terms of the spatial and temporal characteristics associated with the situation.

16. The totality of man's norm definitions is termed his "culture." Inasmuch as definitions are learned through socialization, culture is learned. It follows that culture is social in nature, and is independent of the individual, that is, is learned and would remain even if a particular individual were not present to learn it.

17. Just as humans are capable of applying definitions to objects in the physical world, they are also capable of applying definitions to themselves. The totality of definitions the individual has of himself is termed his self concept or self definition.

18. Humans tend to behave in a manner compatible with their self definition.

19. Since norm definitions are expectations for behavior (Statement 10), and since "scripts" (or expectations for behavior) are typical aspects of roles, norm definitions are characteristic of roles.

20. Because roles are characterized by norm definitions, it follows that they (roles) are an important part of man's cultural definitions.

## NOTES AND REFERENCES

1. ALBERT CAMUS: *The Myth of Sisyphus*, copyright 1955, p. 9. Material reprinted by permission of Alfred A. Knopf, Inc., New York, New York.

2. WILLIAM SHAKESPEARE: *As You Like It, ii*, 7. From *The Works of Shakespeare*. New York: Walter J. Black, Inc., 1937, p. 262.

3. WILLIAM JAMES: *Principles of Psychology*, 2 vols. New York: Holt, 1890.

4. GEORGE HERBERT MEAD: *Mind, Self, and Society*. Chicago: The University of Chicago Press, 1934.

5. CHARLES HORTON COOLEY: *Human Nature and the Social Order*. New York: Charles Scribner's Sons, 1964.

6. JEROLD HEISS: "An Introduction to the Elements of Role Theory" in *Family Roles and Interaction: An Anthology*, J. Heiss (ed.). New York: Rand McNally & Co., 1968, pp. 3-27.

7. GLENN M. VERNON: *Human Interaction: An Introduction to Sociology*. New York: Ronald Press, Inc., 1965.

8. E. A. HOEBEL: *Anthropology: The Study of Man*, ed. 3, copyright 1966, p. 102. Material reprinted by permission of McGraw-Hill Book Co., New York, New York.

9. E. A. HOEBEL: *Anthropology: The Study of Man*, 1966, pp. 102-103. By permission.

10. STANLEY COOPERSMITH: *The Antecedents of Self-Esteem*. San Francisco: W. H. Freeman and Co., 1967.

11. Stanley Coopersmith: *The Antecedents of Self-Esteem*, 1967, p. 120.

12. Theodore R. Sarbin: "A Preface to a Psychological Analysis of the Self" in *Psychological Review* No. 59, 1962, pp. 11-22.

13. Stanley Coopersmith: *The Antecedents of Self-Esteem*, 1967, p. 20.

14. George Herbert Mead: *Mind, Self, and Society*, 1934.

15. George Herbert Mead: *Mind, Self, and Society*, 1934, p. 150.

16. George Herbert Mead: *Mind, Self, and Society*, 1934, p. 150.

17. George Herbert Mead: *Mind, Self, and Society*, 1934, p. 151. By permission.

18. George Herbert Mead: *Mind, Self, and Society*, 1934, p. 158.

19. George Herbert Mead: *Mind, Self, and Society*, 1934, p. 154.

20. C. H. Cooley: *Human Nature and the Social Order*, 1964.

21. C. H. Cooley: *Human Nature and the Social Order*, 1964, p. 184. By permission.

22. C. H. Cooley: *Human Nature and the Social Order*, 1964, pp. 184-185. By permission.

23. Glenn M. Vernon: *Human Interaction*, 1965.

24. Erving Goffman: *The Presentation of Self in Everyday Life*, copyright 1959, p. xi. Material reprinted by permission of Doubleday & Co., Inc., Garden City, New York.

25. Glenn M. Vernon: *Human Interaction*, 1965.

26. Jerry D. Cardwell: "The Relationship Between Religious Commitment and Premarital Sexual Permissiveness: A Five Dimensional Analysis" in *Sociological Analysis* 30:72-80, No. 2, Summer, 1969.

27. Charles Moskos, Jr.: "Why Men Fight" in *Trans-action* 7:13-23, No. 1, November, 1969.

28. Charles Moskos, Jr.: "Why Men Fight," 1969, p. 18. By permission.

29. Charles Moskos, Jr.: "Why Men Fight," 1969, p. 16. By Permission.

30. Glenn M. Vernon: *Human Interaction*, 1965.

31. For a general discussion of the nature of the intersubjective process referred to see Peter L. Berger and Thomas Luckmann: *The Social Construction of Reality*. New York: Doubleday & Co., Inc., 1967.

32. Gregory P. Stone: "Appearance and the Self" in *Human Behavior and Social Processes*, Arnold M. Rose (ed.). Boston: Houghton Mifflin Co., 1962, pp. 86-118.

33. Sheldon Stryker: "Conditions of Accurate Role-Taking: A Test of Mead's Theory" in *Human Behavior and Social Processes*, 1962, pp. 41-62.

And all our Knowledge is, ourselves to know.[1]

ALEXANDER POPE: *An Essay on Man*

# 6

# A PROGRAM
# FOR METHODOLOGY

The perspective utilized throughout this book has been identified as that of the symbolic interactionist. While symbolic interactionism has most often been considered a general theoretical orientation,[2] the discussion presented in the previous pages is more accurately identified as one which attempts to move in the direction of conceptual clarity and, therefore, in the direction of developing a methodology for the symbolic interactionist perspective.

From the perspective of the symbolic interactionist, we are aware of the fact that all humans, including the social researcher, sort out the world of human experience and make it meaningful through the use of symbols. In the conduct of his research, the symbolic interactionist, because he is aware of the symbolic nature of human interaction, does not leave the meaning of the symbols he employs in his research unspecified. As a result, the reader of research utilizing this approach can proceed with the smallest amount of confusion as to what the researcher is investigating. In addition, the specification of the meaning of the symbols he employs aids the researcher in clarifying, for himself, the nature of his research process. Concept clarification and measurement will be our primary concerns in this chapter.

## THEORY AND METHODOLOGY: THEIR RELATION

The degree to which an activity approaches the ideal of science rests in the methods used to arrive at the discovery of general truths or the operation of general laws. Ideally then—from this perspective—it is not *what* one studies but rather, *how* one goes about studying what he studies that is important. There are, of course, some ethical questions as to *why* one is studying something, but we shall not go into that here. Basically, the scientific process is seen as composed of three basic characteristics. These are (not necessarily in order of occurrence or import): (1) science is theoretical, (2) science is empirical, and (3) science is cumulative. Theoretical refers to that characteristic of science which attempts to summarize complex observations in abstract, logically related propositions which purport to explain relationships in the subject matter. Empirical denotes that activity which is based on observation and reasoning, and whose results are not speculative. Cumulative implies the building of theories upon one another, new theories correcting, extending, and refining the older ones (without reference to the consistency condition).[3]

We are concerned with human social behavior, that is, behavior which is evidenced as a result of one individual taking account of, or interacting with, another. We are concerned, then, with the accumulation, systematization, and formulation of knowledge dealing with human interaction. To the extent that social psychology accomplishes this, it is further concerned with prediction. Prediction might, in fact, be termed the goal of any given science.

Braithwaite[4] defines a theory as consisting of a:

> . . . set of hypotheses which form a deductive system: that is, which is arranged in such a way that from some of the hypotheses as premises all the other hypotheses logically follow. . . .

He goes on to state that the theory contains an arrangement from high to low level hypotheses, which are amenable to empirical verification. The problem, however, is the approximation of theoretical definitions to what we desire to "know" through empirical research, and their ease of measurement. In other words, the problem is the relation between theory and research. Blalock[5] distinguishes between theoretical and operational definitions. A theoretical definition is a definition in which ". . . a concept is defined in terms of other concepts which supposedly are already understood. In Euclidian geometry, for example, the concepts *point* and *line* may be taken as undefined (as primitive terms). The notions of *angle, triangle,* or *rectangle,* can be defined in terms of the primitive concepts."

The notion of primitive terms (or concepts) is not as easily illustrated within the language of sociology. If, however, social events exist in a combination of human beings and their associated actions, then it seems reasonable to suggest that we should select primitive terms that represent actors and types of action.[6] If we assume that the ordering of the propositions of a theory is such that one proposition follows logically from another, that is, one proposition can be defined or specified in terms of another, or prior, proposition, then we must assume our theories to be constructed of primitive terms and we can take our lower-order propositions (hypotheses in Braithwaite's terms) as adequate definitions of our terms and proceed to test the hypothesis. Some social theorists consider this to be the case.[7] However, it is rarely, if ever, that we find ourselves furnished with a theoretical definition which is of sufficient specification to allow for precise measurement. The reasons for this are many. One, however, seems to stand out above all others.

The notion of multiple causation seems to deny exhaustive treatment in the general theoretical language.[8] It is true that we are now beginning to circumvent this difficulty with a more precise language of mathematical models, but that is not the issue at hand. The inability of our language to come to grips with the problems of multiple causation usually leads the social scientist into operational definitions, wherein he can specify his procedures used in the measurement of the concept of concern.[9] When the social psychologist involves himself in operational definitions, he does not take certain terms as "understood." Rather, the actual test of an hypothesis is made in terms of the concepts as operationally defined.[10] Further, the gap between the language of theory and the language of research does not seem amenable to rectification in experimental or quasi-experimental research.[11] Thus, when we set out to define our concepts, we define them operationally.

## THE IMPORTANCE OF CONCEPT
## FORMATION AND SPECIFICATION

Concepts, as such, are of little import to the social researcher. We may conjure up any number of concepts and, with devoted attention, introduce them into the jargon of a particular discipline. In general, however, concepts do not represent significant advances in terms of the increase of scientific knowledge. Only when we specify the content of the concepts do they become useful to the scientific community. It should be pointed out that such a statement does not argue for a "raw empiricists" position.[12] It merely states that any concept which does not provide the means for a test of its applicability does not satisfy the basic criterion of admissibility to scientific discourse. The claim then is simply this: Any concept or combination of concepts which does not purport to be admissible to refutation is at least partially unsatisfactory to the scientific enterprise. To admit unspecifiable concepts (whose content can never be known) would allow any concept—sensical or nonsensical—to legitimize itself through an appeal to the consistency condition, which, as Feyerabend[13] has aptly illustrated, is itself unsatisfactory. Concept specification, then, is crucial for the scientific enterprise.

Throughout the previous chapters our analysis has been concerned with the specification of the concepts we have introduced and it has, therefore, centered on attempting to make the concepts methodologically useful. In the process of specifying the content of concepts, we move in the direction of making them theoretically useful. However, the manner in which concepts are specified also indicates to a certain extent the manner in which they will be made methodologically useful—that is, it indicates the avenues available for operational definition of the concepts. This is illustrated schematically in Figure 8.

In social psychology we measure concepts (role definition, self definition, and so on). However, we do not measure our conceptualizations directly. Take the concept of religious commitment, for example. The notion of religious commitment is a theoretical concept, couched in theoretical language (we have already commented on the relation of measurement to language). We may conceive of religious commitment as composed of a configuration of five dimensions (just as we conceived of self definition as composed of several dimensions) —religious knowledge, religious belief, religious behavior (ritual), religious feeling, and the effects of these four in everyday secular life (religious effects). However, these five dimensions remain just that—dimensions—and are not amenable to measurement. While it is true that the five dimensions specify more explicit what we mean by religious commitment, we have gained no additional information as to how we measure the concept of concern. What we generally do then is select or arrive at[14] a set of indicators of each of the five dimensions; for example, church attendance is considered an indicator of ritualistic religious behavior; number of books of the Bible one can recall is termed an indicator of religious knowledge, and so on.[15] The vast majority of studies proceed from here, going through the process of operationalizing and classifying these indicators and measuring the concept of concern. But as Lazarsfeld has commented,[16] this leaves us open to a great many problems. We have no way of knowing if our indicators measure our concept more adequately than any other given set of indicators. Further, assuming that we are indeed trying to relate one concept to another concept, we have no assurance that any given individual or number of individuals has not shifted with respect to one of our indicators while remaining constant, or stable, in terms of the concept we are trying to measure. In other

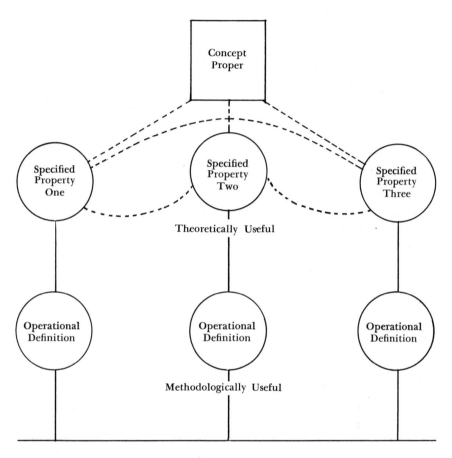

Unspecified Concept

Concept
Proper

Specified
Property
One

Specified
Property
Two

Specified
Property
Three

Theoretically Useful

Operational
Definition

Operational
Definition

Operational
Definition

Methodologically Useful

Research Level

FIGURE 8.

words, there are many confounding influences on the data which our indicators per se may not account for.

Ideally, however, we should go one step beyond the setting up of indicators and arrive at a set of indices. This step involves the combination of our indicators on a given dimension into a single measure of that dimension. Supposedly, then, our index gives a proportional representation of the dimension which we are concerned with measuring. One way of attempting to take care of the confounding influences on the data is to relate our indicators, prior to forming an index, to an outside variable whose relationship to the phenomena we are trying to measure has previously been demonstrated. Lazarsfeld has advocated this method of reducing the probability of shifts in data sources causing confounding of the results.[17] Thus we may find, for example, that several of our indicators relate more closely to an outside variable, say "attitude toward banishment of prayers in schools," than did others. That is, those individuals who express or show strong disapproval of banishment of prayers indicate a higher correlation to strong religious commitment on some of the indicators than do others. (This procedure assumes a previously established relationship between religious commitment and attitudes toward banishment of prayers in schools). In this manner we may rule out some of our indicators prior to forming the index and in the same manner account for some of the factors which are independent of our indicators proper but which, nevertheless, influence their acceptability as indicators. Further, there are methods available for use in experimental situations—depending on the number of experimental and control groups—for accounting for differences in measurement due to the confounding influences of the experimental variable, uncontrolled events, and the after measure.[18] It appears that in the nonexperimental situation, however, the setting up of indices is about as far as we can proceed in accounting for various confounding effects on the data. One exception to this statement is in order. Causal inferences in nonexperimental research can be enhanced by the use of formal mathematical models. This process will be considered later.

## MEASUREMENT

Following Coleman,[19] we define measurement as the use of numbers even without clearly defined rules of operation. This yields us four points on which we may discuss how social science measures its concepts.

Initially, there is that type of measure in social science which allows us to make simple quantitative description. Blalock[20] cites the example of using proportions on a nominal scale. Given that each class we wish to describe quantitatively forms a nominal scale, then numerical descriptions afford us the opportunity to express proportional membership in each class relative to N. The result of all proportions should, of course, be unity.

A second measure in social psychology "is in combination of a number of observations to provide a measure for some hypothetical construct, some inferred property of an individual or a group, such as an attitude or a 'norm'."[21] This involves the social psychologist in measuring indicators as inferring some social property of an individual or group. One example of this type of measurement is represented by the Likert scale.[22] A single question on the questionnaire is assumed to be an adequate indicator (after pretest) of the concept to be inferred. The possible responses to the question (s) run from favorable to unfavorable, with each response assigned a numerical score. The algebraic average of the scores of the individual's responses to all the separate items gives his total score, which is interpreted as representing his position on the numerical scale. The different averages allow us, for example, to make statements regarding differing dispositional states.

A third type of measurement is that which relates two or more quantitative measures of the types discussed above, and the generalization of this kind of measurement usually takes the form of social scientific law. It is true, however, that such measurement is found in social science less often than the first two discussed.

A fourth type of measurement employs the mathematical model. A mathematical theory which seeks to explain and to predict events in the world about us always deals with a *simplified* model of the world—a mathematical model which includes only things pertinent to the behavior under consideration.[23] The application of statistical techniques to measurement of our data in an experimental situation largely allows only the description of covariation between variables, and does not afford the opportunity to make causal inferences. That is, experimental results based on statistical inference involve a symmetry and allows predictive statements in terms of covariation, but not causal ones which are of the asymmetrical form.

Causal statements (ideally) take the form: if X is a cause of Y, we have in mind that a change in X produces a change in Y, and not merely that a change in X is associated with a change in Y. The notion here is that an input into a system *produces* an output. Even "high powered" statistical techniques allow only covariation statements, that is, they estimate a score on a Y variable, given information about scores on an X variable $(X_1, X_2, X_3, \ldots X_n)$. Thus, statistically, we usually cannot talk in terms of cause.

In order to deal with the concept of cause, the mathematical model must be composed of certain simplifying assumptions.[24] Basic among these assumptions is that the model can be composed of a finite number of variables, with unaccounted-for variables (those not included in the system for investigation) taken care of by the introduction of error terms.

While there is symmetry in mathematical equations, error terms allow the utilization of regression equations as causal equations. Further, in order to deal with the variables in such a number that would ordinarily cause equations which do not admit of simple solution, recursive systems are utilized. This allows for causal freedom of dependence of variable $X_1$ on $X_2$, $X_3$, $X_4$. Additionally, in order to satisfy the requirement in recursive systems that there be fewer unknowns than equations, certain of the b's must be set to zero. This allows us to make predictive statements about causal connections fairly easily in a linear relationship. Generally speaking, the technique of the mathematical model involves multiple and partial regression and correlation, wherein by partialing out certain variables we can establish causal connections between the variables remaining in the system. Once this causal connection has been established in the nonexperimental situation, empirical research may be conducted to verify the model.

## GENERALIZATION

Generalization in social psychology usually takes the form of descriptive rather than interpretative statements. Our descriptive generalizations usually define and classify phenomena, make a statement of the empirical relationships associated with the observed phenomena, and simply state *what* happens. If we are to improve our generalizations, we should be able to determine the nature of the observed relationship between phenomena, that is, whether it is causative, structural, and so on. This would entail, rather obviously, some sophisticated techniques for arriving at decisions as to the nature of the observed relationships. It appears, further, that in order to improve our generalizations in the direction of interpretation as well as description, we must develop a mathematical system which is isomorphic with the variables in social psychology, and plug this system into a suitable mathematical model. It appears that only to the extent that we reach this isomorphism between social psychological variables and mathematics will we be able to move in this general direction.

## SUMMARY

We have been dealing with the present state of measurement in social psychology, and with its associated difficulties and problems. How we should measure our observed phenomena has already been implied, if not spelled out. The answer is the development of a mathematical symbol system which is isomorphic with what our concepts indicate. A second answer, which almost presupposes an adequate mathematical system, is computer simulation of human behavior. It would aid us in

104

circumventing many of the problems of controlling for unknown effects of unknown variables. As Colby,[25] has stated, "A computer model states very explicitly what a belief is, what conflict is, what anxiety is, or—rather than 'is'—what or how these elements are represented in a language the computer can process. Computer models provide a way of rapidly coming to decisions about alternative organizations of highly complex systems. Finally, they have properties of versatility, subtlety, and evolving growth, which make them appropriate models for mental and social processes."

## NOTES AND REFERENCES

1. AUSTIN WARREN: *Alexander Pope as Critic and Humanist*. Princeton: Princeton University Press, 1929.

2. See, for example, ARNOLD M. ROSE (ed.): *Human Behavior and Social Processes*. Boston: Houghton Mifflin Co., 1962.

3. GLENN M. VERNON: *Human Interaction: An Introduction to Sociology*. New York: Ronald Press, Inc. 1965.

4. R. B. BRAITHWAITE: *Scientific Explanation: A Study of the Function of Theory, Probability and Law in Science*. Cambridge: Cambridge University Press, 1955.

5. HUBERT M. BLALOCK: *Social Statistics*. New York: McGraw-Hill Book Co., 1960, pp. 9-11.

6. HUBERT M. BLALOCK: *Social Statistics*, 1960, pp. 9-11.

7. HANS L. ZETTERBERG: *On Theory and Verification in Sociology*. Totowa, New Jersey: Bedminster Press, Inc., 1965, pp. 52-54.

8. HUBERT M. BLALOCK: *Causal Inferences in Nonexperimental Research*. Chapel Hill: The University of North Carolina Press, 1964, p. 5.

9. PAUL F. LAZARSFELD: "Concept Formation and Measurement in Behavioral Sciences: Some Historical Observations" in *Concepts, Theory, and Explanation in the Behavioral Sciences*. Gordon J. DiRenzo (ed.). New York: Random House, Inc., 1966, p. 11.

10. HUBERT M. BLALOCK: *Social Statistics*, 1960, p. 11.

11. HUBERT M. BLALOCK: *Causal Inferences*, 1964, p. 5.

12. See ABRAHAM KAPLAN: *The Conduct of Inquiry*. San Francisco: Chandler Publishing Co., Inc., 1964.

13. PAUL K. FEYERABEND: "How to Be a Good Empiricist" in *The Philosophy of Science*, P. H. Nidditch (ed.). New York: Oxford University Press, 1968, pp. 12-39.

14. For a more sophisticated treatment of the manner in which indicators are selected, see any text on factor analysis.

15. See, for example, J. E. FAULKNER AND G. DEJONG: "Religiosity in 5-D: An Empirical Analysis" in *Social Forces* 45:246-254, 1966.

16. PAUL F. LAZARSEFLD in: *Concepts, Theory, and Explanation*, 1966. p. 190.

17. PAUL F. LAZARSFELD in: *Concepts, Theory, and Explanation*, 1966, p. 187.

18. CLAIRE SELLITZ, ET AL.: *Research Methods in Social Relations*, New York: Holt, Rinehart & Winston, 1961, p. 110.

19. JAMES S. COLEMAN: *Introduction to Mathematical Sociology.* Glencoe, Ill.: The Free Press, 1964, p. 86.

20. HUBERT M. BLALOCK: *Social Statistics,* 1960, pp. 25-26.

21. JAMES S. COLEMAN: *Introduction to Mathematical Sociology,* 1964, p. 8.

22. RENIS LIKERT: "A Technique for the Measurement of Attitudes" in *Archives Psychology* No. 140, 1932.

23. J. R. PIERCE: *Symbols, Signals, and Noise.* New York: Harper & Row, Publishers, 1961, p. 45.

24. HUBERT H. BLALOCK: *Causal Inferences,* 1964, pp. 27-60.

25. K. M. COLBY: "Stochastic and Computer Applications in Free-Association" in *Mathematical Explorations in Behavioral Science,* F. Massarik and P. Ratoosh (eds.). Homewood, Ill.: Dorsey Press, 1965, p. 117.

# NAME INDEX

107

# SUBJECT INDEX